Real Estate

How to Get Rich in Real Estate Without Owning Physical Property

(Getting Your First Sale and Achieving Long-term Success & Proven Marketing)

Federico Teague

Published By **Ryan Princeton**

Federico Teague

All Rights Reserved

Real Estate: How to Get Rich in Real Estate Without Owning Physical Property (Getting Your First Sale and Achieving Long-term Success & Proven Marketing)

ISBN   978-1-998927-31-9

No part of this guidebook shall be reproduced in any form without permission in writing from the publisher except in the case of brief quotations embodied in critical articles or reviews.

Legal & Disclaimer

The information contained in this book is not designed to replace or take the place of any form of medicine or professional medical advice. The information in this book has been provided for educational & entertainment purposes only.

The information contained in this book has been compiled from sources deemed reliable, and it is accurate to the best of the Author's knowledge; however, the Author cannot guarantee its accuracy and validity and cannot be held liable for any errors or omissions. Changes are periodically made to this book. You must consult your doctor or get professional medical advice before using any of the suggested remedies, techniques, or information in this book.

Table Of Contents

Chapter 1: Basics of Real Estate Investing

Each new investor should have a robust know-how of investment basics. While constructing a strong basis is honestly vital to create financial stability, wealth, or acquire retirement desires, building an amazing foundation in real assets making an funding will offer the same advantages.

When it consists of investments, on the equal time as there are fantastic shared traits among real assets making an investment and further traditional methods much like the stock marketplace, mutual fee range, or municipal bonds, there also are a massive form of variances. While you will be nicely familiar with terms together with move returned on investment (ROI), yield, or dividends, it's miles however possible to revel in concerned while you're provided with unexpected phrases like internet strolling earnings, cap rate, or seasoned forma.

Let's start via taking a while to test a few actual estate investment requirements, so one can assist you get a firm footing as you input the area of actual property making an investment.

Why do people invest within the first place?

By placing money into an investment account, you can create or complement your profits, which may be carried out to increase your nest, growth your economic savings account, and assemble monetary protection a long manner into retirement.

While Social Security is useful for masses humans, many others won't have enough profits to stay to inform the story thru retirement or won't have Social Security in its modern shape for the long time. In that case, you can want to put together for the possibility of a further supply of profits in the destiny, and this could help you financially in retirement. To start saving coins and building that nest, simply set apart a bit each pay period and earn interest at the difference. The faster your coins will increase, the bigger the go back you'll acquire.

A large percent of buyers have portfolios that contain severa investments which encompass stocks, bonds, and real belongings, and some just invest in shares and bonds. Although the large speak over which investment is higher, it certainly is actual assets, is difficulty to strong opinions, no person can deny that real property may be a precious asset to an funding portfolio, and the reality that actual belongings:

- can offer ordinary passive income

- has the functionality to understand or boom in charge through the years

- gives you with the capability to use as debt surety to elevate your internet shopping electricity and cross again on funding

It furthermore has the capacity to generate huge returns, beginning from eight to fifteen percent.

While making an funding in any form of asset beauty has hazard, most of the hazard associated with actual property making an investment may be minimized via a cautious pre-investment due diligence method. Now, let's examine the severa options for making an investment in actual belongings.

Investing strategies for real estate

With regard to the problem of passive rather than lively investment, you may put money into real belongings passively, because of this you are a passive participant and are not chargeable for managing the property or funding yourself; or actively, in which you are an energetic participant and are answerable for acquiring, handling, and getting rid of the property.

Passive Real Estate Investing

Passive investments are higher suitable for oldsters which can be willing to commit plenty tons much less time to their investments, as they do no longer call for the identical quantity of daily involvement. In favored, energetic investments usually will be inclined to have extra fees of move decrease again. Prior to growing an investment in actual estate, make an effort to evaluate some time desk to determine how masses time you may dedicate on your real property investment endeavors. Determine the funding type you're maximum cushty with to suit your available time and desire for engagement.

Passive investments generate an income circulate termed cash go with the flow, it really is frequently provided inside the form of condo income or dividends. Income in the shape of passive property, consisting of hobby, dividends, and capital income, is taxed in a special way than normal profits, and loads of human beings pick out to earn this shape of income.

It isn't always unusual for consumers who've commenced making an funding to desire to branch out of the stock marketplace and diversify their portfolios with the aid of the use of making an funding in real assets. While it could appear tough to interact in actual assets, there are however remarkable options to participate in real property through REITs and ETFs.

REITs

A Real Estate Investment Trust (REIT) is a company whose stocks have a particular designation, and they'll be presented and owned with the resource of a set of buyers who every pool collectively a certain sum of money. That coins is once more to investors in the shape of a dividend as a way to pay at the least 75% or more of all earnings made. REITs may be publicly listed or privately traded, and traditionally they've got had a great song file.

Investing in REITs is a clean remember. It best requires shopping stocks from a brokerage account for a few hundred bucks. While there are fundamental lessons for REITs, the overall types of REITs encompass fairness REITs and loan REITs, though, it's miles possible to discover CRE businesses that serve a outstanding kind of commercial enterprise actual belongings (CRE). Compared to creating an funding in stocks, making an investment in REITs is pretty smooth and allows even those who've minimum financial belongings to start making an funding in actual estate.

ETFs

An Exchange-Traded Fund (ETF fund) works in a similar manner to a mutual fund, but as opposed to in fact investing in mutual finances, the fund invests in actual belongings-related commodities like REITs. The fund supervisor selects individual REITs to invest in, which gives buyers who collect stocks within the actual assets ETF the capability to diversify their portfolio holdings for the duration of numerous superb CRE sectors and with numerous special REITs.

If you have were given a brokerage account, you could buy a actual assets ETF for as little as a few hundred bucks, making this an splendid access funding.

Crowdfunding

Investors which might be searching for to put money into actual estate can check out taking aspect in a crowdfunding platform that connects a sponsor, the lively partner within the business commercial enterprise employer, with finances from numerous buyers. A pretty appropriate funding possibility is professionally dealt with with the aid of way of the sponsor and the sponsor's body of workers, who assure an investor an above-common move once more over a positive time period. When an investor invests in a crowdfunding undertaking, he might not be capable of get proper of entry to his coins for a while. That manner he'll want to pay a penalty to get his cash returned. While it's far viable to earn a outstanding cross lower lower back thru using utilizing crowdfunding as a passive investment, it does consist of threat.

Real estate that is for apartment purposes

In condo actual property, month-to-month hire is amassed and profits are produced as a stop end result. Unlike in a project in which you receives a fee for the hours you parent, a landlord gets month-to-month cash glide, irrespective of the reality that she or he does not should spend the identical amount of hours to gain this. The condo earnings is consistent. Although your earnings source want to potentially be a solid one in retirement, you want to maintain an eye fixed fixed on the apartment bills if you want to maintain to generate strong coins waft in the long term.

If you're trying to hire a residential assets, like a unmarried-own family home, apartment, or triplex, you may do so or you can select to hire a industrial enterprise property, collectively with an administrative center, commercial building, retail center, or rental complicated.

The IRS believes condominium income is passive, but an investor stays concerned due to the truth he or she have to participate in lease sports activities to benefit the monetary advantages of proudly owning the belongings. Investors have a large obligation thinking about that they must research, display, and manipulate each funding possibility; moreover, they ought to have identify and possession for the property, which incorporates identifying to shop for taxes and coverage, as well as making vital protection and upgrades.

In terms of management, the more passive or lively a condo assets is, the extra critical it is. If you hire a 3rd-party control commercial enterprise business enterprise to undertake continuing manipulate for you, they will contend with it. Alternatively, you could deal with it your self. When it comes to condominium homes, the priChloe attention is the amount of labor required. What elements have an effect on your investment alternatives is a complicated question, that would best be answered after you've got investigated a number of capacity investment opportunities.

Residential real estate is a famous beginning component for logo spanking new shoppers due to the reduced prematurely fees making it an easier entry issue. In many situations, getting a loan for a $100,000 unmarried-own family residence is less difficult than receiving a business mortgage for a $one million enterprise building. Commercial houses are assessed in a unique way than residential homes, which means it's miles essential as a way to differentiate among numerous forms of condominium real property in order to select out which funding plan is the fantastic in shape for you.

High-circulate lower again private equity fund

A non-public equity fund collects capital from a number of customers and invests that money in real belongings property. The manipulate and their employees are responsible for allocating and managing investments, giving consumers a preferred circulate lower back or dividend on a month-to-month or quarterly basis. Commercial actual assets investments may be made in privately-held non-public fairness rate range, which spend money on commercial organization actual assets, residential actual belongings, and actual belongings debt like appearing or non-performing loan notes.

For a length of time set via the non-public equity fund, investment fee variety deposited in that fund are illiquid, because of this that the investor is not capable of get his or her coins out of the fund with out incurring a penalty. Security Exchange Commission (SEC) regulations require personal fairness finances to pool their cash steady with sure recommendations and are not to be had to the overall public.

The exercising of drawing mortgage notes

You aren't definitely making an funding in real belongings while you invest in a loan word. Instead, you are making an investment inside the debt that backs up the belongings.

Just as a monetary organisation will beautify finances to accumulate a belongings, an man or woman may additionally boom finances to accumulate a domestic. To meet a monetary duty, a property consumer symptoms and symptoms a phrase and mortgage making positive to repay the debt and makes a monthly fee to the lender, whose proceeds function both the maximum crucial and interest rate.

In this example, the investor earns passive earnings within the shape of cash go together with the flow as long as the borrower is making ordinary payments.

Passive Real Estate Investing

Active actual belongings investments contain active participation at some stage in everything of the investment. An vital difference to undergo in mind is that real assets funding frequently acts like a business employer, wherein only profits are acquired in case you are actively strolling at the assets. Rental actual property is classified as passive because it depends on the control, but it could be deemed an active real belongings investment if the owner chooses to recognition on tenant enhancements.

Fix and flip

With a restoration-and-flip investment, you purchase a assets, make modifications to beautify its rate, and then promote the property. The purpose of this technique is to revel in the assets by using using selling it. The investor wants to have energetic management talents to effectively turn a house. They might also even want to deal with negotiating a reasonably-priced buy charge for a property, doing the maintenance themselves, or supervising and handling the contractors to finish the artwork. Fix-and-flips can be a excellent technique to make a massive sum of money in a short length of time, but they're taxed on the pinnacle end of the tax bracket because it is a quick-term capital benefit.

Wholesaling

Buying in bulk (or wholesaling) is the act of performing the vital research and basis to find an unlisted or undervalued opportunity, negotiating a completely cheap purchase rate, and then assigning that agreement to a wholesaler (client) at a instead higher rate. The wholesaler makes a rate from the distinction a number of the agreement some of the seller and the patron, and the settlement between the customer and the seller. When it includes beginning as an active real property investor, wholesaling is an smooth manner to get started out because you truly need a bit sum of money. While you want to installed plenty of time, it is not now not viable. The handiest way to earn coins is to be a wholesaler when you have a sales possibility pending.

Person-to-character quick-time period rentals

In evaluation to prolonged-term rentals, which can be additionally referred to as excursion rentals, quick-term leases, which consist of tour rentals, are normally leased for a nightly or weekly duration. An more and more well-known short-term renting choice is short-time period rental services like VRBO and Airbnb, which allow belongings owners to rent out a bit of their domestic or the entire residence. When a assets is applied in a quick-term rental manner, it should be provided and maintained with the useful resource of the property proprietor, which incorporates checking interior and out the tenants and cleaning the assets on the result in their live.

When it involves brief-term leases, it may be more worthwhile than extended-time period leases, however however, it's far more inconsistent. The price of vacancy is associated with wherein the belongings is located and the decision for for excursion or brief-term rentals within the region. During seasons of excessive vacancy, apartment property proprietors ought to make massive income, even as for the duration of intervals of excessive occupancy, proprietors want to dedicate big time to operations. Before identifying to hire space in your home or to buy a vacation rental, make certain you understand the applicable community guidelines and rules so that you recognize if you may legally provide a quick-term condo on your city or county. Many cities have rules or license requirements which is probably precise to them.

Real property investments and tax deductions

Because actual property is taxed in a specific manner based totally clearly at the form of assets you personal, it's miles essential to assess your alternatives for purchasing and promoting assets earlier than making an investment in real estate. A REIT's dividends are taxed otherwise than the ones of normal stock dividends. Additionally, apartment real assets is taxed in a considered one of a kind way than a healing-and-turn investment technique may be. If you put money into actual belongings tax-unfastened or tax-deferred, you could earn extra earnings. You need to recognize how your own home funding(s) will effect your taxes, counting on wherein you live, earlier than shopping for your first piece of actual assets.

To take the plunge, or no longer?

Investing is constantly unstable, even though there are some assurances. No depend in that you location your cash, whether or not or now not, with a financial manual, the S&P 500, or in actual assets, your investments may be significantly strong. However, there can be commonly the opportunity that you can lose your coins or get a pass again this is less than what you planned. With asset allocation, you could diversify your portfolio at some stage in a couple of actual estate techniques, but it is no matter the truth that viable to take risks with investments. Before you're making any funding in real belongings, you should determine your hazard tolerance and hold to finish your due diligence on numerous funding alternatives, so you can become privy to which real belongings funding method is appropriate for you.

Remember even though, the wealthiest human beings inside the international have earned their fortunes in numerous techniques, however one commonplace element connects masses of them: they have got executed real property as a essential issue in their making an investment plan. When it involves all the strategies the extraordinarily-rich made their fortunes, actual estate finished 3-to-1 better than all of the others.

Do you want to additionally make investments like the wealthiest humans inside the international? If so, hold studying to discover the satisfactory possible manner(s) to accomplish that.

In precis...

• Each new investor must have a solid information of funding basics.

• Passive investments are higher suitable for parents which can be willing to devote tons less time to their investments, as they do now not name for the identical quantity of every day involvement.

- In wellknown, lively investments have a tendency to have greater prices of pass once more.

- When it comes to brief-term rentals, it could be more profitable than long-term rentals, however rather, it's extra inconsistent.

Chapter 2: Finding the Perfect Real Estate Investment Niche

Investing in real estate may be very complex. However, one of the most extensively typical portions of recommendation to buyers of each age is to discover a specialised area of interest inside the real belongings marketplace. For instance, possibly you're asking what exactly a real assets location of interest is. To find out real belongings niches, I've developed a guide. In this monetary ruin, you could see the severa sorts of niches available to clients, the elements you could need to think about whilst choosing a gap, and what it way to be a successful investor.

Rental of houses remains the maximum popular actual assets funding location of hobby. Rents hold to rise in the unmarried-circle of relatives home condominium enterprise, with many real assets markets displaying will boom of three-five% or more. And for many years, the housing inventory has now not saved up with call for. Such situations can provide super capability for traders who very non-public real belongings with condominium yields.

For people with an interest in actual property, what is a real assets niche?

A area of interest additionally can be a term which means a specialized region of know-how. Often, real property investors are searching for to popularity their investments in a specific region, which they do to restriction their losses. This is in particular actual for consumers who are new to the market and have not but had the opportunity to diversify their portfolios. It is, despite the fact that, the case that even the most seasoned investors may additionally additionally have as a minimum one section of the real property area they love.

While the definition of a real belongings investing vicinity of interest differs from that of a actual property funding method, each have similarities. To positioned it another way, on the same time as a actual property funding approach is the manner you earn cash in real belongings, a gap is the specific investment vehicle in which you perform that method.

A applicable concept for a person who wants to hire out residential real belongings homes to long-term renters could be to put into effect a purchase-and-keep approach in real property and consciousness on renting unmarried-own family homes. At the identical time, a person who pursues a repair-and-flip technique may moreover purpose houses located in growing organizations with economic issues.

Real belongings has terrific niches

The actual belongings marketplace has severa first-rate alternatives that permits you to pick from. I've performed the hard be simply proper for you and indexed a number of the severa opportunities that I've decided. This isn't a whole listing, but it need to come up with some mind to hold in thoughts at the same time as searching out new subjects to get into.

1. Property-related niches

The outstanding distinctiveness you would in all likelihood consider as a real belongings investor is focusing on a great assets type. Among the maximum well-known funding property types are:

●   Dwellings occupied through a unmarried family

●   Multifamily dwellings, which consist of duplexes, triplexes, and quadplexes

- Apartments and condominiums

- Duplexes

- Land in its natural state

2.   Commercial actual property specialization

While this may seem uncommon, the difference is essential since it indicates the kind of person that lives in residential and business corporation houses. In comparison to business actual estate, commercial real property has a few particular capabilities. Beginners must generally avoid it. However, my distinctive e-book is going over the approach of making an investment in business company real belongings in remarkable element. If you are inquisitive about making an investment in industrial real assets, there are a number of alternatives that allows you to pick out from:

- Space for retail

- Office area

- Industrial region

- Self-storage facility

- Industrial-allocation land

- Real property investment trusts (REITs) (EFTs)

In both of the two options above, you can pick out to popularity on a selected section of the usa of the usa, metropolis, or city. However, in case your entire portfolio is invested in a unmarried actual belongings marketplace, and there may be a downturn, it may make an effort on your property to go back to their previous cost.

Finding the proper place of interest is a essential next step once you have got were given a better hold close to of the numerous actual belongings niches. By simplifying the way, I actually have reduced it into severa smooth steps:

1.   Real assets funding niches can't be determined until an investment purpose is ready. You will in the end choose the way you desire to invest based totally on your funding dreams.

2.   The next degree in choosing an available and feasible actual belongings funding fund is to choose an investment plan. Many elements have an impact on making an funding choices, but considering the opportunities in your marketplace allows you 0 in on possibilities.

3.   To prepare a sturdy marketing strategy for putting in vicinity a real belongings employer, make certain to carry out sizable studies. Before choosing a specialization, you want to discover all of your possibilities. It is constantly an terrific

concept to test the listing of specialties above, to make certain now not some thing has modified. Speaking with an professional within the actual property making an investment profession for your vicinity is a extraordinary way to advantage similarly steering.

Weighing the professionals and cons

Now it is time to investigate the whole thing in each location of interest so you can end up better acquainted with everything to be had. The actual property market has precise blessings and drawbacks for every business enterprise.

While this can now not be exactly actual, buying expensive real property almost commonly outcomes in a better pass once more. In evaluation, the up-the front cost is higher. As a surrender give up end result, you can not be able to transact the identical quantity of transactions at a discounted pricing variety.

Once you've got determined how an awful lot you are willing to invest, you need to then decide whether or not or not or no longer or not you're willing to accept the accompanying dangers and advantages. As a cease result, pick out your course of action. If you have got had been given very well investigated all your alternatives, you could have all the know-how you need to determine which marketplace area is proper for you.

Additionally, take into account: a real belongings area of interest isn't always "set in stone". Choosing a career you detest does no longer need to be an option. It's flawlessly brilliant if you'd need to test with a particular one. You might possibly find a 2d place to make investments in case your funding portfolio diversifies.

All in all, to sum it up, proper here are the takeaways. Looking into a specific place of actual property will can help you form a path for your future investments. Take this example drastically, and anticipate it through carefully.

In precis...

●   Rental of homes stays the most famous real assets funding location of interest.

●   Rents preserve to upward push in the single-family   home   condominium organisation, with many actual estate markets displaying will increase of three-five% or greater.

Chapter 3: Finding Good Deals on Properties

You can be looking to put money into actual property for quite a few motives: you may want to make investments to pursue your lengthy-time period desires, or you may be just starting out and searching for to construct your portfolio. Regardless of your goals, starting out may want to require finding the extraordinary offers for your network. If you can accomplish it, you're in a high-quality function for achievement nowadays and within the future.

When it entails opportunities, you have to search for them, in area of look ahead to them to find you. You can discover actual belongings investment possibilities by means of manner of being tough-running and informed. It's no longer a game of risk. If you are able to keep up, you could generally win.

While using a actual belongings agent to let you come to be aware about residences for sale can be a superb idea, it can not be the nice manner to move about it. Or are there better offers being sold and purchased with the resource of the usage of folks who are right now involved in the real property industry, and we do not know approximately them? Yes, and there can be an answer.

So, start thru thinking about of the notable techniques for latching without delay to profitable possibilities in your neighborhood vicinity.

Gaining a monetary earnings through the usage of

When it entails investing, don't take a seat down on your arms searching ahead to three issue to drop for your lap. Instead, take to the streets and search for houses in neighborhoods of hobby. "Driving for bucks" is our time period for this tactic. While you're visiting, you need to keep your eyes peeled for two exquisite varieties of residences, FSBOs and distressed or deserted houses. Let's speak about each the kind of.

1.   FSBOs (For Sale By Owner)

These houses which can be listed with the resource of proprietors with out a real property agent, or as "in the market thru proprietor" (FSBO), include a minor element of the marketplace however are automatically disregarded by way of way of big game enthusiasts. You have the liberty to make your personal choices on what to do subsequent. It's that smooth.

All you have to do is hop on your vehicle, power spherical your vicinity, or investment region, and search for opportunities. Be it for sale with the resource of the owner, you are superb to look an FSBO domestic made sign on nearly every market. This indicates that a property owner is interested by selling, however hasn't however been indexed by using using a real property company.

One manner to do this is to take a photograph, be aware down the mobile cellphone range, or method the house and knock on the door. You need to do the whole lot to your power to lock down those reductions. In addition to that, you could furthermore keep away from paying an agent's rate because of the reality you're maximum likely able to negotiate a straightforward good buy.

2.   Properties in distressed or abandoned state of affairs

When you be aware homes that appear in disrepair or are vacant, pay interest. Disheveled homes have their appearance and definition in common with misery homes, meaning that each houses have a extreme need for protection or are forsaken or abandoned. Generally, as the amount of difficult work a property calls for will boom, the leverage you want to barter better discounts will growth.

The following are a few first rate identifiers that suggest a belongings has been abandoned or is in a country of misery:

• A mailbox that is overflowing with letters

• An abandoned building internet website online with a code violation label

• Boarded up home domestic home windows or doorways; or shattered home home home windows or doors

• There isn't any meter area, or the draw near switch is off

• Long, uncut grass and shrubbery

- A roll of tarp on the roof

- A lot of rubbish, junk, or waste inside the the front of the residence

In most times, a house will seem unkempt or abandoned for the cause that there is often a genuine purpose. For example, inside the case of the seller, if he's now in foreclosures, what's he presupposed to do subsequent? It's viable that they took care of the house for years, and now they can't due to their negative monetary situation. No remember quantity range how difficult the promoting environment is, you're almost great to have seen a delivered about issuer. Stop one-of-a-type customers from getting there first, and you can have an top notch funding for your fingers.

You may additionally discover a assets that appears to be abandoned or in distress but without a dealer statistics or absolutely everyone inside the house. In this example, write down the address of the belongings. You ought to have a look at the street cope with and the quantity of houses opposite and adjoining to it.

With that during mind, have your home are searching for completed on Google or Zillow.Com so that you can begin investigating the matter. Zillow.Com will supply vital records, like the call of the assets owner, the variety of bedrooms and lavatories, the square photos, whether or now not or now not it is in foreclosure or pre-foreclosures, and their contact statistics. Or you may ask the friends of the property in a pleasant manner. This commonly saves time and yields high-quality outcomes if finished gently and with politeness.

Once you have got received an intensive facts of the assets, you'll be able to provide you with a progressive method to take it. A easy instance can be if a assets modified into in foreclosure. You can be allowed to the touch the financial group to make an offer in advance than it's miles placed up for auction.

If the house is physically distressed and unkempt, you'll first attempt to find out the proprietors. Once you locate them, you may try and get in contact with them via the use of SMS and call until you get through to them and may make a proposal. You may be able to get the proprietor's smartphone quantity the usage of whitepages.Com, with a purpose to make looking loads simpler. To sort of estimate, a number one rule of thumb is to call 3 times, and no greater in order no longer to agitate the vendor and lose out on the future deal.

In addition, you may want to use electronic mail to touch them. Convey that you're a real assets investor with the aid of way of writing a sincere letter describing your buying approach: that you got homes outright, for coins. You have to moreover offer step-via using-step commands at the way to preserve if they are interested by selling. Include your internet website or a phone quantity to name, so others can contact you. If you have not however brought the letter, ensure to vicinity it in the mailbox or at the front door.

Going a step similarly, you could knock on the door and spot if everyone is domestic. Do no longer be scared to introduce yourself to the house owner and provide an cause for what you do in case you are given a solution.

"Hello, I'm a close-by actual property investor within the location, and I'm interested by shopping numerous homes in this avenue. Do you have got your house on the market? Do you apprehend of absolutely everyone else in the community who has their assets available on the market?"

Lest we overlook approximately about, you are making a large bounce with this. Some doorways gets slammed to your face, will they now not? Yes, of path. However, if you may weather the typhoon, you're nearly advantageous to get preserve of many treasured "yeses". And this is usually nicely statistics.

The bottom line is that this approach can bring about outstanding costs, in spite of the truth that the house proprietors aren't actively seeking to sell.

Word-of-mouth marketing and advertising

Acquiring real property additionally can be finished with phrase-of-mouth marketing. Word-of-mouth is one of the fantastic strategies for locating superb real property gives. Make truly every body aware about your intentions. It's usually an splendid concept to approach your friends, partner and kids, buddies, and buddies, and allow them to realise which you're looking for to build up an investment assets or two.

It is vital to have a look at that real estate making an investment isn't a lonely game. There is someone handy who's considering promoting their home, is ready to promote, or is in a jam and desperately wants to get out. If you may be the solution to their problem, if you could get a assets off their fingers, there may be a great possibility you could choose out up an splendid belongings for a brilliant fee.

Word of mouth is notable in view which you have the opportunity to behavior transactions with sellers earlier than they listing their houses to be had in the marketplace.

Say, as an instance, that Uncle Peter located out that the subsequent-door neighbor Chloe had customary a new advertising and could be transferring to every other country. It may be essential that she unexpectedly sells her home. It is obvious Uncle Peter is privy to you want homes, so he offers Chloe your touch statistics.

Chloe tells you that she has to relocate in a rush, and she or he or he asks you to maintain her deposit steady. With the records you provide to Chloe, she is aware of you're a actual belongings investor who purchases houses with coins and closes speedy (which brings a smile to Chloe's face).

Now you be conscious what surely befell, do not you? It's beginning to appear like there might be a deal in the works.

You can also chat with distinct people on your place who're well-informed about the regions and neighborhoods in which you live. It is probably all people, whether or now not it's miles an prolonged-time period resident, the mailman, or someone who makes regular deliveries within the location. Stay-at-domestic moms who even take their infants on every day walks may additionally show beneficial.

They can function your eyes and ears, constantly keeping a watch out for any signs and symptoms of capability—some rogue strands of grass and a stack of papers heralding an deserted residence, an FSBO signal that regarded in a single day, or a touch of network communique which suggests that the neighbor is transferring to Florida.

Have an instantaneous courting with them. Let them recognize that you're at the quest for tremendous offers and that you have what you're attempting to find in mind. These men will allow you to apprehend whilst there are excellent gives at the horizon.

Putting all of it collectively

Tick the box of everybody you understand, and then plant the seed. Make a unique try to look your community for FSBOs and distressed houses to search for listings "this afternoon". As your recognition and facts of your trouble increases, you have got got a better danger of outbidding others and securing a exquisite deal earlier than sincerely everybody else receives a chance.

Picking up the ones excellent gives is step one in growing your funding portfolio and your long-time period riches. Finally, it's time to get available and begin seeking out your first or next top notch investment property.

In summary...

- Tick the sphere of all people you understand, and then plant the seed.

- As your hobby and records of your problem increases, you have a better hazard of outbidding others and securing a extremely good deal in advance than actually every person else receives a threat.

Chapter 4: Top Features of a Profitable Rental Property

Rental investments may be interesting and sincerely profitable in case you make the proper alternatives. But past the income and the gratification of your ego, investing in actual estate can be daunting for a primary-time investor.

Too many questions, too many doubts, too many fears. This is why it is critical to do in-depth studies earlier than embarking on the journey, to apprehend all the blessings and disadvantages of your actual estate condo funding.

Here are the most critical elements to consider at the same time as looking for worthwhile actual property to invest in:

1. Location, Location, Location

It is a dependancy of pro investors to think about the vicinity as golden.

The neighborhood in which you buy your condo, constructing, or residence will decide the sorts of tenants you entice, your rent, and your occupancy charge. The location no longer exceptional makes it viable to hire to many tenants but additionally to plan for exceptional kinds of leases with the condominium returns that go together with it. If you are searching for close to a college, there can be a fantastic hazard that students will dominate your ability condominium marketplace, and you may have a tough time filling your gadgets even as the university is on wreck.

A shared tenancy is likewise an choice to keep in mind inside the ones conditions and makes it viable to boom the rents.

2. Property tax

Property tax varies masses depending in town and place you're making an investment in, and also you need to realize how a amazing deal you may pay. You additionally want to understand the dynamics of property tax within the place you want. High belongings taxes are not usually a horrible difficulty, but they do now not recommend the outstanding of life in a particular community or avenue. Some unattractive locations nevertheless have a excessive assets tax despite the fact that. You can get statistics from the metropolis making plans branch of your municipality or region of preference.

Make sure you find out if assets tax will increase are in all likelihood in the close to future. The consultation with pals is important on this experience. Increases in assets taxes are possibly in conditions:

1.   If taxes have no longer or little advanced for years,

2.   If the property tax will increase frequently each 12 months through a percent better than inflation.

A metropolis in financial problem can decorate taxes properly beyond what a landlord can moderately charge for hire.

three.   Schools / Colleges / High faculties

Consider the pleasant of nearby schools if you are renting homes with multiple mattress room for couples with children. Also, at the equal time as you're particularly involved with month-to-month rents, the overall price of your rental investment kicks in while you do emerge as promoting it.

If there aren't any right colleges close by, it can have an effect on the charge of your investment and restrict the capability for capital gain.

4.   Security

No one wants to stay next to a crime and delinquency hotspot. The municipal police should have accurate statistics on crime within the neighborhoods in that you want to make investments. Exchange, speak, construct relationships with the police. Check the fees of vandalism, extreme crimes, and minor misdemeanors, and make certain to observe whether or not or not crook interest is developing or lowering. You also can discover approximately the frequency of police presence for your network with a community survey.

Another way to stumble on a problem within the community is to have a have a look at the evolution of actual estate fees in the place over severa years. If they will be decrease than inside the relaxation of the city and keep taking region...run away.

5.   Labor marketplace

Places providing more and more employment opportunities appeal to extra tenants. It makes experience, however you continue to must do a little research. To find out how a selected vicinity has the deliver of jobs, seek advice from the internet site of the National Institute of Statistics.

If you note an industrial about putting in a massive business enterprise inside the vicinity, you may make sure that personnel looking for a place to live will flock there.

This can result in better or decrease house prices, and rents, depending on the kind of enterprise worried. You can count on even though that if a massive industrial organisation moves to a metropolis, tenants will too.

Conversely, if employment in a locality is basically based on a unmarried massive industrial business enterprise business enterprise, your rental funding is likely to be depreciated if it moves.

6. Leisure and enjoyment opportunities

Take a excursion of the community in which you are thinking about a rental investment and discover all the elements of a pleasant dwelling environment that attracts tenants, together with:

- parks

- ingesting locations

- sports halls

- cinemas

- public shipping

- vacationer attractions

The town hall or tourist place of work can also have promotional substances which can provide you with an concept of in which the first-rate stability is amongst public infrastructure and domestic areas.

7.   Future development / Potential for Plus Value

The metropolis planning department may need to have records on developments or initiatives and machine which is probably to return decrease returned into the place. If there is lots of manufacturing taking place, this might be a high-quality growing area. Watch out for state-of-the-art homes that might lower the charge of surrounding homes. Also, be aware that many extra gadgets want to compete collectively along with your condominium funding.

Conversely, infrastructure collectively with a tramway or a highway front is a very great sign for the future improvement of the price of your own home.

eight.   Number of advertisements and the emptiness charge

If a network has an specially immoderate extensive form of listings, it may signal that it is a community in decline. Unfortunately, immoderate vacancy prices pressure landlords to lower rents to draw tenants. A low vacancy charge permits landlords to growth rents.

This is the not unusual feel of supply and contact for, what we name Yield Management.

nine.   Average rents

The apartment income might be your deliver of income, so that you want to understand the minimum not unusual rent of the neighborhood or the road in which you make investments.

Don't smile, that may be a certainly common   mistake   with   seasoned consumers who have a tendency to accept as authentic with their lucky stars too much in preference to the numbers. Make positive that your condominium funding can with out problem generate sufficient month-to-month hire to cowl your:

- mortgage

- community taxes

- different current fees

Do enough studies at the location on the manner to check how it's going to evolve over the following 5 years.

If you may have sufficient money to buy a property in the vicinity in recent times, but taxes had been to rise, a property that is low price nowadays could lead you to monetary disaster later. You need to consequently continually preserve in thoughts an negative state of affairs for your marketplace studies, so that you can be organized for any terrible improvement.

10.   Natural failures

Insurance is a few other fee that you'll be wanting to subtract out of your rents, so you want to understand how an lousy lot it will fee you. And specially, in no manner reduce lower back on coverage.

Insurance typically charges more and more each day, but it saves your existence inside the event of a tough blow, like water or fireside damage.

If a city is vulnerable to landslides, thunderstorms, hurricanes, tornadoes, or floods, the expenses of proper insurance can but considerably erode your condominium earnings.

We skilled an earthquake and a few homes on the edge of the municipality have in no way been covered via manner of coverage due to the truth the municipality as a whole had too few claims even as the houses involved had been very close to the epicenter!

Obtaining reliable data

To better invest your cash in "stone", it's far vital to analyze all the essential statistics in your funding. The expert resources are thrilling, and I virtually have mounted you ten tips above to help you bypass in addition (or stop a future deal) if vital. But you'll have to talk to the friends to get real hints. Talk to tenants and landlords alike. Tenants might be a whole lot greater honest approximately the negative factors of a community due to the reality they have got now not invested in it so there may be no sentimental attachment.

Visit the community at unique instances of the day (and even greater interesting at night time), and on one-of-a-kind days of the week to look your future buddies.

Choice of rental belongings

The nice real assets investment for novices is often a single house or a condo. Condominiums require little preservation because of the truth the condominium supervisor appears after the upkeep in the commonplace and structural elements (which incorporates the roof), which leaves you the priority only of the indoors of the lodges to prepare for the tenants. However, condominium residences usually tend to earn decrease rents and recognize greater slowly than single-family houses. Single-circle of relatives homes also tend to draw longer-time period tenants. Families or couples are also often visible as higher renters than unmarried people due to the reality it's miles believed that families may be more financially strong and pay hire frequently. It's an opinion even though...

Determining the rent

How is the capability lease determined? You will need to make an informed estimate. Don't get over excited through overly optimistic assumptions. Too immoderate a lease and an empty home for months rapid reduces your normal profits and your real property cash glide.

Start with the common network lease and paintings from there. Ask yourself if your own home is properly absolutely really worth a hint extra or a chunk less than commonplace, and why. Improve the tool and decoration of your provided condo to cause a overwhelm and obtain a better rent. To find out if the rent amount is right for you as a real assets investor, calculate what the assets will in reality fee you consistent with month in preservation fees and taxes and deduct the minimal lease from it. From there, you may recognize whether or now not your investment task is profitable sufficient or not.

The essential takeaways

Every area has accurate cities, every city has suitable neighborhoods, and every community has right streets. Every avenue has nuggets for a worthwhile condo funding.

It takes an entire lot of paintings and research and visits to align all the elements that determine a splendid rental investment with high profitability.

When you have got determined the best property, have realistic condominium expectations, and ensure your charges are healthful enough that you can sit up for the belongings to begin earning income with out dreading any emptiness at any time of the 12 months.

In summary...

- A low emptiness fee lets in landlords to increase rents.

- Single-family homes additionally have a tendency to draw longer-time period tenants.

Chapter 5: Cash vs Financing

Many customers wishing to make economic investments in the actual belongings location are in search of advice from me often. Usually, they've got huge capital: among $100k and $750k. But they would really like to have data at the approach to undertake. They hesitate among paying coins and borrowing.

Indeed, the financing of the condominium investment is completed in two techniques: the investor can pay coins alongside alongside together with his very personal financial belongings or borrow the whole amount crucial for the operation. The mortgage also may be a partial amount of the general sum.

The cash rate has blessings. The investor gets all of his hire as soon as his investment is made. It is exempt from reimbursements, the danger of non-reimbursement, banking fees, and formalities. It is therefore blanketed from the pressure associated with these types of operations. But he's obliged to have the whole amount desired to buy coins. And that money is locked in till the go back on funding is complete. In addition, given the bulk of charge variety to position at the table, the investor not regularly has the coins for other responsibilities.

Despite all of the uncertainties related to borrowing, its monetary hobby is commonly effective. In truth, apartment funding with leverage makes it possible to gather the assets without committing the investor's non-public fee variety. This exercise allows the latter to get wealthy through the use of the cash of others. You can boom capital via debt. Your available cash stays intact and can be directed to distinctive initiatives. In the occasion of dying, your death coverage reimburses your mortgage, which protects your family. And your heirs get hold of in reality bought real property.

In view of a number of those opportunities, need to we select out the coins rate or the mortgage? Take a quick observe the subsequent:

1. Interest on credit score

Taking out a home mortgage remains the exceptional manner to finance a condo funding. Logic: credit score has a leverage impact. It lets in you to become the owner of a assets this is more tough to pay cash for. You can therefore finance housing whilst putting your budget in one of a kind topics. Note that condo assets is the most effective funding that may be financed with a mortgage. Banks may not lend you cash to shop for stocks...

2. A profitable funding

A 2d accurate cause to finance a condo actual assets funding on credit score score score: the hobby price of the loan is most usually decrease than the gross price of flow again for your actual property funding. If you add capital profitability to apartment yield, the overall net profitability is greater than the price of your loan. In quick: you are a beneficiary.

three. Optimized taxation

Third argument: loan interest is deductible from rents even as you declare them for tax. You because of this lessen your tax base, which optimizes your taxation. In addition, mortgage loans are almost commonly related to lack of lifestyles and incapacity coverage, which secures the operation.

Nowadays, the phrases of the loan are suitable. The techniques related to credit rating score are smooth. And financial organization fees are low. For over decades, I without a doubt have received a mortgage at a rate of 1.Fifty 5%. The life insurance fee, within the meantime, is amongst 2.Five% and 3% over the identical duration. It is therefore mathematically greater interesting to make every a monetary funding in existence coverage and a mortgage for condominium purposes. With regard in your funding in life insurance, you have got were given a wonderful argument to offer in your banker as a purpose to supply you the loan.

The preliminary steps getting financing for your own home

Before embarking head-on inside the look for investment, you need to reflect onconsideration on defining your challenge and ask yourself the query: what do I actually need? House or condominium or land that I can gather some component on? These questions should permit you to outline your specific need after as a manner to allow you to examine your looking for functionality. This buying functionality allows you to determine how hundreds you want to make investments and borrow. It consists of your borrowing capability similarly to your personal contribution that is typically needed to cover guarantee and notary expenses. Once your assignment has been decided and the finances you need to dedicate to it, you may then begin your financing studies.

1.   You sign a agreement to shop for a property

You have discovered your home and made a purchase provide which has been common. The next step is to move beforehand with the signing of the cause to buy the record.

This income agreement is an genuine act that commits you and the seller to finish the sale of the assets in a condition and at a hard and fast rate. The income settlement can also encompass a suspensive clause that determines the most date by way of which financial institution financing need to be received. This duration can typically be 30 to forty five days from the date of signature of the compromise. The patron advantages from a right of withdrawal of ten days which he can exercising with out a want to justify it. If you do not gain financing in advance than the forestall of the suspensive clause, the sales agreement might be canceled.

The specific desire is word of mouth. This differs from the signed file as it most effective commits the vendor to reserve the property for a destiny customer through agree with. This is commonly done in instances where the seller does now not thoughts going with you to the monetary group.

2.   You acquire the assisting files in your financing document

These files relate in particular on your:

- personal situation

- credit score rating

- monetary situation

- property or your internet sincerely actually really worth

- modern-day loans

- unique real assets projects

They are crucial for bankers because it allows them to rapid put together your document and certainly to exactly examine your situation to offer you with the most suitable solution on your undertaking.

three.   Send your financing request to numerous banks

You must negotiate and accumulate for yourself the brilliant fee. Together, with the bankers, find out a tailor-made financing answer that lets in you to take benefit of flexible and brilliant conditions concerning, for instance, reimbursement closing dates or results.

4.   You accumulate the settlement

After a have a look at of the files submitted, the monetary institution will speak to you its agreement in writing. If your request is common, it is vital for the continuation of your challenge. This agreement, in precept, is a record submitted through your monetary institution which confirms its willingness to hold with the strategies. It is in no manner the popularity of your mortgage software program. This settlement makes it feasible to set particularly:

- The loan quantity

- The credit score charge

- The time period of the mortgage

- Guarantees

- Conditions

In positive instances, this settlement can be located via the phrases "hassle to similarly evaluation". This factor out does now not officially dedicate the monetary group to the provide this is proposed to you, it shows that the financial institution will ask for an in-intensity assessment of your document:

- Further records about your present day debt degree

- Statement of economic institution bills

- Personal contribution

The analysis of your report and the findings that emerge from it will right away impact your mortgage software program and could as a end result allow your lending business enterprise to go earlier contractually or no longer with you. This self-discipline will then materialize in what is called a totally final settlement. Thus, the contractual mortgage record specifies:

- Your identity and that of the lending enterprise business enterprise

- The inclinations of the mortgage mortgage: Amount, period, private contribution

- The reimbursement phrases

- Guarantee and insurance fees

- General and unique conditions

five.   You signal the mortgage provide

The contractual loan document issued through the lending monetary group seals the right provisions of your financing. The loan offer is legitimate for a length of 30 days at some point of which the monetary employer cannot regulate the conditions of the offer. To be legitimate, the provide must be normal after a minimum duration of reflected image of 10 calendar days. Before the expiry date of the offer and after the reflected picture length, you will therefore need to move back the signed loan offer to the economic institution to signify your agreement.

Be conscious that once you're taking out a loan with a financial institution, the latter may additionally moreover ask you to open a bank account to domiciliate your income with them in element or in complete.

6. You sign the deed of sale with a notary

The signing of the deed of sale is the closing step to formalize the real estate transaction. Carried out via way of a notary, this record confirms the records gift inside the settlement which consist of touch information, trends of the property, obligatory diagnoses, fee, notary charges, or guarantees. Beforehand, the ones numerous statistics are tested thru the notary. After the price range have been transferred, the deed of sale can be registered with the resource of a notary and you will gather your name deed and keys. You, consequently, emerge as the owner of the belongings which you were coveting for a few months.

For introduction paintings, the rate variety can be released as and while the work progresses.

7.   You very non-public and pay off your loan

You take benefit of the property received and start repaying your first month-to-month rate both one month after signing or deferred in step with the situations set through your loan.

In summary…

•   Interest on credit score rating Taking out a home mortgage stays the wonderful manner to finance a rental funding.

•   A loan loan is nearly continually associated with dying and incapacity coverage, which secures the operation. It is therefore mathematically more interesting to make each a monetary investment in life coverage and a loan for apartment abilties.

•   Together, with the bankers, discover a tailor-made financing answer that allows you to take gain of bendy and effective situations regarding, as an example, reimbursement deadlines or effects.

Chapter 6: Real Estate Financing Options

Obtaining credit score at the same time as not having to go through the services of a monetary group is viable. Indeed, for numerous years, the services which suggest to bypass the conventional banking intermediation multiply. Here is a pinnacle degree view of the specific solutions available to you if you need to carry out a undertaking using others' credit score with out going via a economic organization.

To perform a mission, whether or not or not or no longer it's miles the acquisition of a automobile, the financing of a journey or even work in your house, you could want a mortgage. Indeed, in case you do no longer have the crucial economic savings apart, borrowing and repaying over the years is an incredible answer.

Soliciting economic institutions (banks or specialized credit score agencies) is often the number one reflex for customers. Logical, because the banks pay interest maximum of the loans granted these days. But one-of-a-kind possibility answers are rising to assist households.

Loans between people have extended, however additionally crowdfunding permits fine initiatives to be achieved. In addition, there's furthermore microcredit, which lets in human beings excluded from the conventional banking system loans in severa international locations so that you can borrow.

Borrowing without a bank is consequently possible, every out of responsibility for people who can not gain loans from conventional banks or by using choice, for folks who want to examine up with an middleman.

Is getting a economic group credit score rating practical?

Securing financing for real belongings homes on the dimensions required is one of the maximum essential for any actual belongings development challenge and therefore for every developer. One of the crucial abilties of real estate is its immoderate capital depth. Since real property is an costly commodity, its purchase or advent requires a large quantity of capital funding. Raising budget for the purchase or production of a real property object is, on the only hand, an crucial measure, and on the opposite, an detail of the formation of the profitability of returns on such an funding.

The effects of the theoretical check concerning the assets, techniques, and sorts of financing real property gadgets confirmed the subsequent:

• Both the extensive sort of financing strategies and their composition range.

- There are tremendous lexical variations in the names of financing strategies.

- Often the varieties of financing differ little from the methods.

Thus, we consider it expedient to unmarried out the techniques of financing, and in them - the styles of financing, which encompass sources of financing.

 Funding Methods

 Funding Method Features

 Self-financing

 Financing virtually from very private charge variety

 Shareholding

 Financing thru transactions with stocks and other securities

 Loan financing

Financing on the phrases of payments

Consortium financing

Financing through combining possibilities with super commercial enterprise company entities

Leasing and selling

Financing now not in coins, but with owned fabric on certain situations

Concessional financing

Financing on phrases which may be substantially more profitable than the ones gift in the market

Subsidizing

Financing on a no-cross again foundation

Blended finance

Financing via a aggregate of severa financing strategies

Lending cash immediately among individuals is likewise possible. This isn't, moreover, a novelty. With own family or pals, it's miles possible to lend each unique coins.

For the US marketplace, there are 8 capacity actual property financing answers to be had that do not include banks.

Portfolio Loans are the primary shape of mortgage.

In evaluation to conventional mortgages, portfolio loans aren't resold at the secondary market to massive economic institutions which includes Fannie Mae and Freddie Mac. So in place of being compelled to obey the rigorous tips imposed via using the secondary client, creditors are given the freedom to set some thing phrases they deem suitable. Portfolio loans, in place of ordinary mortgages, can be tons much less complex to gain for shoppers and self-hired borrowers because of this. Because maximum creditors who deal in portfolio loans do not publicize their services, it is critical to are seeking out a lender thru recommendations, investor networks, and other approach. Otherwise, you'll in reality need to touch every lender and inquire right away as to whether or not or now not they offer portfolio loans.

Federal Housing Administration Loans are the second one type of mortgage.

When it includes mortgages held through banks everywhere in the united states, the Federal Housing Administration is involved, and furthermore they offer a software application to assist human beings in shopping homes wherein they anticipate to live completely. As a stop end result, an FHA-sponsored mortgage does not apply to "investment belongings" within the strictest experience. The exception clause, however, permits you to utilize an FHA loan to shop for a home with as tons as 4 devices in case you live in most effective considered considered one in all them, in keeping with the FHA. The truth that this form of mortgage calls for a minimum down fee of tremendous three.Five percent is the primary attraction.

203K Loans are the 0.33 type of mortgage.

In maximum areas, a 203K loan is identical to an FHA mortgage in phrases of its terms and conditions. It varies from the others, despite the reality that, in that it lets in you to borrow extra price range to use in rehabilitation and healing duties. This more money is protected within the right real estate financing, which makes it extremely smooth.

Owner Financing is the fourth opportunity.

It is feasible to avoid highly-priced economic organization fees and make payments right away to the house owner if you may discover a home owner who owns his home outright, desires to sell, and is ready to provide the financing. You will nearly without a doubt must pay a higher interest price, but the transaction can be completed extra speedy and without issue.

Hard Money Loans are a sort of loan that is difficult to gain. It is however feasible so it is our 5th alternative.

A "difficult coins" mortgage is made by way of the use of way of a private industrial company or investor, instead of a bank, for the aim of making a quick-term financial funding. These loans, however, deliver a excessive degree of hazard, supplying buyers with the possibility to make a short earnings via flipping or refurbishing worthwhile homes.

Furthermore, because of the fact hard cash loans are normally treated fast, they make it less complicated to accumulate such assets earlier than it's far too past due. It may be determined whether or now not or not or no longer to offer the loan based at the assets's market genuinely worth, in area of primarily based on collateral. The interest fee is more than commonplace, starting from eight percent to fifteen percent, with a time span starting from 6 months to 3 years.

Personal Loans with Confidentiality is the sixth possibility.

These loans are much like hard coins loans, besides that the lender and borrower have a greater private dating with each other. Because of this dating, it's far less difficult to attain an agreement on situations which can be suitable to every events, and the hobby fee, factors, and costs are frequently appreciably much less highly-priced. If the borrower fails to satisfy his or her commitments, the lender also can despite the fact that foreclose on the assets.

Home equity financing is the 7th preference.

Taking a home fairness mortgage is often extra handy than utilizing for a extremely-modern mortgage in case you already private a bit of real property and feature built up terrific equity in it. This may be in the form of a loan (HEIL) or a line of credit rating (HELOC), and banks are commonly willing to really take delivery of you when you have a big quantity of fairness constructed up in your property. The financial group will first-rate lend a set percent of the general value of your present day assets, minus the quantity you continue to owe on that assets, commonly 90 percentage of that rate. This is often enough to cowl at the least a part of the down price on the new assets you're considering. You may be capable of deduct the interest you paid at the mortgage out of your taxes as well.

Commercial Loans are wide range eight on the listing.

Other than residential real estate financing, the alternative seven techniques said above can also be hired for commercial actual property finance, which can be very worthwhile. A business loan will generally have a higher price of interest and fees, in addition to a shorter compensation period. For commercial actual property flipping, a business business corporation line of credit score is each other option to take into account. While the profits degree of the borrower is generally the maximum critical approval requirement for special types of loans, the sales that the assets is deemed able to producing is the most vital interest for enterprise loans. Your financial skills in addition to your preceding enjoy in the scenario of commercial enterprise actual assets investment is probably substantially reviewed as well.

Crowdfunding to avoid banks is the ninth choice.

Another manner to keep away from banks, crowdfunding. If you need to perform a personal task that could hobby one among a type humans, then you can ask for help, along with financial participation! When the compensation occurs within the context of crowdfunding, we name it crowdlending.

With crowdfunding, it's miles even possible for some human beings to make a capital or fairness investment, this is to mention, to take shares within the venture or the organization financed with the help of crowdfunding.

The collection of financial donations as a loan is the tenth choice.

While first of all, most crowdfunding systems allowed participants to suggest tasks with a social or solitary measurement, today it is simple to provide all obligations. A non-public venture, a real belongings undertaking, the advent of a begin-up, or the financing of a adventure...nearly whatever goes.

Many obligations are consequently financed manner to donations, with none compensation. It is on occasion possible to offer a praise, with a present, a promotional object, or perhaps a thanks symbolically.

In summary...

● Obtaining credit score without having to go through the services of a economic employer is feasible.

Chapter 7: Real Estate Investment Strategies

R. Kiyosaki said: "I do now not want to promote my belongings, I want it to supply me coins every month, over and over another time." Our project can be to discover as a bargain as possible such homes that allows you to supply us no longer a one-time earnings, but a consistent, monthly, annual, hundred-12 months, thousand-one year profits, without our participation. This is our intention!

Real belongings is continuously growing in rate. In 2022, 2030, and 2050 real property will grow in charge and generate profits! You can see the statistics on the boom of actual assets fees global. People are although shopping for flats, houses, land plots, and plenty of make massive fortunes in this. Will you be among them? It's as much as you to decide!

Many of the techniques mentioned on this chapter paintings in every increase and bust. But our challenge isn't genuinely to shop for and sell, our challenge is to shop for and get preserve of cash from a property for lifestyles. Buy-promote hypothesis is not the superb device, as it's far regularly related to market dependence. It can also show to be an entire lot riskier than the ones we will communicate approximately under.

Important be aware! These strategies may be mixed, superimposed on each other, introduced as a part of one to a few exceptional, address severa without delay, in levels, all of it is primarily based upon on the way you see this organization. There is usually a method to boom earnings and decrease expenses. The crucial element in all this is to recognize that there can be no perfect technique, the principle issue is to do it. Better to do fairly, however do, than do not anything nicely! Remember this.

Enough terms, allow's get right right down to industrial organisation!

Strategy No. 1. Purchase - Renovation - Sale

This approach is surely this sort of as a way to allow you to make cash as fast as feasible, capitalize your income, and enter some exclusive, more worthwhile assignment. This technique can be used as a hard and fast of the money supply.

How to sell with out cash? Example: You discover a pal, accomplice, investor, offer him to shop for an apartment. It may be an old condominium, "killed", or a new building that wishes protection. Doing preservation along with your very own arms or by using using hiring personnel. In a month you give up the belongings and get 50% of the distinction (income) in coins.

Several such homes and you can already purchase an condo at the facet of your non-public cash. These can be new houses, secondary housing, or vintage homes. The important aspect is to apprehend the scheme itself. We take without repair - cheap, we sell with restore - high-priced! Here you may moreover make some of studios out of it or rent it daily and share the profit with the investor (the best who gave you the money). The crucial problem isn't to forget approximately to attract up all the agreements with a notary really so later there may be no scandals at the same time as you're asked to head away. Always reassure the whole thing.

The downside here is that you may mess with the finances and now not meet it. The crucial detail in all strategies, anything you do, is the miscalculation, tracking, and attempting out of the market. I can even contact in this challenge rely in addition.

Strategy No. 2. New homes

At the diploma of the inspiration, there are certainly cosmic reductions, installments, mortgages. Having presented an condominium at the improvement degree, the rental will fee you an awful lot a lot plenty less than the same in the finished model. The promoting technology moreover may be achieved here, even at a few stage inside the improvement segment. In without a doubt 1 twelve months, a assets can growth in fee numerous instances. Many are engaged in buying and promoting on this region of hobby.

What strategies need to you operate? You additionally should purchase at a miles a lot much less complete degree then, you could watch for the very last touch of the development and hire it, dividing it into studios. You can lease it every day, make a hostel, if this is the floor ground, then you could switch the property to a non-residential fund and hire the condo as a store.

There are drawbacks right right here. The first is that you need to attend as a minimum a year for the building to be constructed and placed into operation. Second, the reality that even as you count on the improvement, the property may be frozen and then it will become a headache, and now not a commercial enterprise employer. Carefully pick out out a depended on and reliable builder who does not have issues.

Strategy No. Three. Alteration of an condominium to a mini studio

The purpose of this approach, regardless of whether or not you've got got an condominium, a residence, or a townhouse, is the maximum division into studios and next hire. This method is one of the profitable ones. We have a chunk, we divide this piece into small quantities and hand them over. If we upload cash from small pieces, it seems a high-quality deal more than if we give up a whole piece.

For instance, a one-room condominium can deliver, say, 3,000 greenbacks consistent with month, if we divide it into studios, then we get at least 2, frequently even three studios. So we will hire a smaller studio for 1,800, and a few different big studio for 2,000 dollars. In fashionable, we get 3,800 bucks. If we manipulate to make a few other zero.33, then this is every different 1,500 greenbacks. Total: we get 5,3 hundred bucks from an condo divided proper right into a studio, in desire to a few,000 greenbacks from the entire condo! This is 2,three hundred greenbacks consistent with month greater than they rent in the marketplace. This is +27,six hundred dollars in keeping with one year of extra money. And if you have severa such residences?

With this technique, the loan goes well. Example: So if we buy an apartment on a mortgage and pay 3,500 greenbacks from it each month, and we get 5,three hundred dollars from renting out the studios, then this mortgage is paid not through you, however through the tenants, plus you earn 1,800 bucks on top. And when you have numerous such houses or houses?

Strategy No. Four. Unfinished

If you efficaciously calculate and bend the owner properly for a reduction, pointing out the dented jambs, and so on, then you can make a respectable coins flow. Different strategies may be completed proper right right here. You could make studios and lease them out, you can make a hotel, rent it out for rent, or make a hostel.

You can use crowd-investing (public funding) or pooling (equity participation) and cease constructing a residence with someone else's cash and fingers. You can live on one of the floors, and rent the relaxation. This is without a doubt a part of what you could do, use your imagination and calculate the whole thing.

The disadvantage which could get up is to miscalculate the repair and very last touch. This isn't always a cheap commercial enterprise, so calculate the whole thing straight away so that you recognize in which each dollar you need to spare will move.

When we arrived inside the town of Denver, Colorado Region, there has been a 2-tale unfinished building close to our residence. It stood there for approximately eight years. I do not understand how prolonged it stood in advance than that, however the element is that during 2014 it turn out to be sold out and finished. Now it's far a tire provider and a vehicle preserve. Judging by means of what type of motion there can be all of the time and the fact that a person is using the location and, being a employer, renovates it all of the time, we are able to finish that the consumer made the proper preference with the selection of purchasing the dilapidated place. It's best to appearance that this constructing is now operational and not a bottle and rubbish warehouse.

Strategy No. Five. Transfer from residential to non-residential

The approach is especially useful for oldsters which is probably engaged in their private enterprise and growth it, looking for a cheap condominium area or, in fashionable, for this area to be their personal. There is likewise an entire business enterprise right here.

You can use the method to lease out premises to special businessmen. In such premises, you may frequently see shops, proper here you can moreover join all varieties of greater premises, making the assets huge.

Here, you should purchase a massive room, with immoderate ceilings, with the opportunity of completing the second ground, developing the location, and because of this the earnings as a minimum two times. The critical detail proper here is to discover an area appropriate for settling human beings. You ought to make hostels, premises for cafes, dormitories for university youngsters out of such houses. You can mixture techniques. Again, it all relies upon on what's available to you - what you see. It is then as a exceptional deal as you to squeeze coins out of every meter as plenty as viable. Basements are sometimes used for hostels. If you embody hobby and creativeness, then you can moreover see that money is literally below your ft.

The drawback of this approach is that it could take time and in addition cash, but if you have a fixed, then that is all solved and alternatively fast.

Strategy No. 6. Large places of work to mini-offices

Like Strategy No. 3, dividing the place of work gives us extra income than if we rented it in its entirety. In famous, any approach with dividing a massive one right right into a small one and then selling or renting small parts of it offers extra profits. Whether it's shopping for cars and selling them for components, or dividing a organization into stocks, or shopping for in bulk, promoting at retail, this approach is as vintage due to the fact the area. Buy a huge one, cut up it into many small portions, and you could have extra profits.

Here you can moreover have a look at the technique of subletting the premises with the consent of the proprietor to demarcate his premises. Then it's going to value you even an awful lot much less, and the internet profits will be made faster, without using more (your) coins.

The downside of this technique is super that you need to find out a appropriate vicinity in which there is a name for for offices, as well as preserve in mind the dimensions of the redecorate, but if there can be a set, then you could usually find out people who will do it for you.

Strategy No. 7. Office with the useful useful resource of the hour

Now that we have were given divided the places of work, you may lease a number of them for an hour or extra. As with dividing region, dividing the time of change also makes extra cash than absolutely lease for a month. This applies to both homes, houses, and business organisation real belongings. Everything that can be divided - we divide, the entirety that can be handed over and take greater for it - we embody!

In order to apprehend how this works, we are able to use an example. Here we've had been given an workplace, it is able to deliver four,000 bucks a month, we hire it by manner of the hour (for negotiations, commercial organisation meetings, and so forth.), as an instance, an hour will value 50 greenbacks, which can be very little. But permit's calculate that the workplaces work 22 days, 10 hours each, out of these 10 hours we take eighty% (with enough advertising and marketing) and multiply thru 22 days. 22 x 8 = 176. Now we multiply 176 (that is a month) hours via manner of 50 bucks normal with hour, 176 x 50 = eight,800 greenbacks! Not terrible math, do no longer you settle? The distinction in delivery monthly and hourly is 4,800 greenbacks! This is fifty seven,six hundred bucks consistent with three hundred and sixty five days from best one place of work rented with the aid of using the hour. And if you have severa of them?

The downside of this method is in putting in advertising and marketing as you want a consistent float of customers. You also need a crew that will help you with the organizational paintings with clients.

Strategy No. Eight. Daily sublease of houses

A big plus of this technique is that you could start with out your very very own houses and with minimal investment. I apprehend those who started out out this actual estate business employer with this method with out making an funding whatever in any respect, and it works.

The approach is easy, we hire an rental on a monthly basis (for a protracted length) with the right to sublease (the right to re-hire it to others) and rent it out with the aid of the day. Having hired the important body of workers, you do no longer want to be present in this enterprise company in any respect, even apartments may be looked for and released without your participation. It all is based upon at the setup of the device. The profitability of this industrial company can be as an entire lot as two hundred% normal with month! You can commonly discover tenants seeking out short-time period stay via net websites like AirBnB, Expedia, and inns.Com, and so on.

There is excellent one minus right here, in locating customers and adjusting for the eternal occupancy of houses. Having set this up, you may not should worry approximately the settlements anymore and could most effective need to growth the wide form of houses, getting extra and more money.

Strategy No. Nine. Dorms and hostels

Here are the hostels, honestly without a doubt really worth considering as a business enterprise business enterprise version of the future. Hostels rule! This isn't always actually an area wherein you could throw the cube like college youngsters, it's miles an entire community, a get-together of travelers, progressive humans, individuals who are interested in finding new friends and spending time with interesting sports activities. The hostels have the Internet, all communications, all device, an area for board games, and most significantly, every hostel has its very personal more sights round its vicinity that lure human beings like a magnet. Now the problem of pill lodges has started to increase, these also are hostels, but at a one-of-a-type level.

Remember, I stated that dividing the space and time into separate portions gives more earnings, and so, hostels are the maximum profitable of these divisions, right here you can place a 3-tiered mattress on two rectangular meters and earn greater from 1 rectangular meter than from daily lease or transport of mini offices via way of the hour.

The drawback of this approach is in locating suitable premises and its tool. Good investments also are required, however if there may be a approach, a group, and an investor, then you can usually do the whole thing with someone else's hands and cash, getting a piece of the industrial corporation. The essential difficulty is to effectively calculate the whole thing, check and installation the method, bringing it to the end result! There are heaps and lots of dollars in this approach!

Strategy No. 10. Townhouses, duplexes, quad homes

It is critical to calculate everything here, in principle, as a few one-of-a-kind area. The fundamental idea of purchasing a townhouse is that it is a turnkey residence and the price section is pretty excessive, which means that that clients who will hire a house are geared up to pay. Here, the method of dividing into studios and renting for a long time, daily hire, can be moreover related to the house, thereby growing your income. You can lease a issue and stay in the identical house. You can offer you with outstanding alternatives with extra abilties, as an example, the Internet, parking for which humans are inclined to pay. The mortgage approach additionally applies right right right here. The rent for housing might be enough a notable way to cowl the mortgage and so that you have more than one hundred greenbacks left each month.

The downside of the method is that it requires a reasonably large get entry to for the cash. If you use a mortgage, then everything will come out an awful lot less expensive. The number one issue is to calculate the entirety so that you do now not run and frantically search for cash. Connect your companions, buyers, and, of direction, your head!

Strategy No. Eleven. Country belongings

Many people assemble groups in this method. Suburban actual belongings is in demand and could increase as cities grow. A moment comes whilst the metropolis starts offevolved to develop tiresome and a person is seeking out wherein to relaxation, to be closer to nature, but without giving up the benefits of civilization. This is wherein organisation starts offevolved for you.

The device is simple, purchase inexpensively, divide into studios, connect or sublet and rent. Around nature, similarly from noise. Ecotourism. There is a name for for this, and it keeps to develop. In famous, ecotourism is a brand new direction for many humans and you may make cash on it. Houses can be bought not tremendous outdoor the metropolis but additionally near seashores and motel areas.

This business enterprise is for folks who need to be some distance from the town and on the equal time do commercial organisation. For such people, this approach is proper. Again, right right here you may blend one-of-a-type methods of renting, subletting, dividing, outbuildings, and various things, you need to calculate everything and look at the terrain.

The disadvantage of this system is, of course, in the clients. The charge of houses out of doors the city is small, however the most critical aspect is to discover ways to trap a super patron go with the waft. If calculated successfully, this may provide an amazing earnings and hundreds of top notch emotions, and if this house is owned someplace at the seaside, then it's far definitely extraordinary. I should have lived there. Yes. Take unfinished buildings in inn areas, hire, and stay there. Take motion!

Strategy No. 12. We assemble a reasonably-priced residence, speedy and share

This is the sort of strategies that our family and group regularly implement. I genuinely like it, and now I will allow you to apprehend why.

I love to create, I want to make candy out of garbage and promote it for additonal than what it grow to be in advance than. Or, to place it some other manner, do approximately the sector-famous Peugeot ad in India? If you don't, I'll will let you recognize.

A younger Indian drives as lots as an elephant in his vehicle. The car can be very antique. And so he sits within the cabin of his automobile and looks at a picture of a modern Peugeot (Peugeot 206) after which begins offevolved. He crashes the automobile into the wall within the the front, then reverses, then he locations the elephant on the automobile in the proper places, and voila, he has a present day Peugeot 206, or almost new...

If you do not know what I am speakme about, then type within the YouTube are trying to find bar: Peugeot 206 commercial enterprise - India. The advertising and advertising and marketing may be very revealing.

So, the construction of reasonably-priced homes might be very just like this industrial, with the handiest distinction being that we're capable of have pretty exquisite houses, and we are capable of rent them above market price because of the vicinity and beauty of the interior, exterior, and services furnished.

This approach is mixed with many, here you could buy land anywhere (the precept detail is to calculate the earnings), you can build from used port packing containers, foam plastic, adobe (a mixture of clay and straw), and so on. By the way, the latter method could be very environmentally best, so I have to advocate anybody to live in houses and lift their children in them.

After production, we launch the residence and lease it out, each day, monthly, or as a hostel. If you pick out out the proper area (near the metropolis), then you can continuously have 100% occupancy, and the income is genuinely cosmic.

This commercial enterprise agency is without issues scalable and simply creative. Here your task may be in deciding on the land, what the residence is probably like, a manner to make more profits with the useful resource of constructing a massive residence that covers maximum of the land plot. It's a incredible method and I find it irresistible.

There is only one minus proper right here, in that creation calls for cash, but once more, by means of the use of attracting traders and the right people who are prepared to go into proper into a percent, you may right away put together capital for yourself.

The introduction and commissioning of any such residence can take approximately a month, which may be very cool, thinking about that the sooner we release a business organisation, the quicker it pays off and starts offevolved to preserve us a profits.

Strategy range 13. Overseas assets

With this approach, you do not need to be terrified of economic crises in your home u . S . A .. You can excursion and stay in your very non-public residences. This is a top notch method for diversifying your portfolio, wherein you may have not most effective actual property for your place of origin, however furthermore, say, Thailand, India, China, UAE, UK, Spain, Greece, Bulgaria, Cyprus, Turkey, or perhaps Brazil.

Such real property can yield income every from 100% consistent with three hundred and sixty five days and from a hundred% in step with month, relying on the vicinity and your strategy. The global locations that I indicated above in the meantime are well-known for investment, if you can not sit nevertheless, then take this method and skip in advance, overcome the global locations! Here, further to with one-of-a-type structures, you may do company both on advent, and on delivery, and on sublease, in addition to in one-of-a-kind techniques. By switching to your mind, you could discover coins, humans, and all of the assets.

The downside of this technique is that in the usa of the us in that you have an funding belongings, there can be a struggle, disaster, or distinctive, then it's going to no longer have a excellent impact for your company. But from any scenario, you may continuously discover a way out and gain, therefore, calculate the whole thing and increase your investment approach.

Strategy No. 14. Auction homes

This is a cool technique in which you should buy land, homes, flats for extremely low fees. By the way, not quality houses however additionally tool, cars and an entire bunch of numerous matters, even loans. Knowing the manner it in reality works, you may use all of the techniques on the aspect of this one. If wherein and what to search for, and what it may deliver, then this will come up with a large gain over different businessmen and traders.

In summary...

● You have to make studios and rent them out, you may make a hostel, and so forth., In 2022, 2030, and 2050, actual belongings will develop in price and generate earnings!

Chapter 8: How To Prepare a Successful Real Estate Business Plan

All businesses (companies, corporations) want a marketing and advertising technique. This bankruptcy is prepared real assets business corporation plans, about the problems related to its improvement. It is a beneficial help for readers who're without a doubt going to create a modern-day-day actual estate company, in addition to people who are not new to the company however need to growth its scope, alter or supplement the tips of their sports.

A actual property marketing strategy is a making plans report. It is critical, irrespective of the whole thing, planning is a system of innovative know-how of the destiny of your business enterprise (agency). At this time, you decide: wherein route to growth your company and the manner brief, a way to gain your desires and what to do to reduce possible surprises and dangers, a manner to control the situation as an entire. In different phrases, effective making plans is the method of putting goals (desires) and growing sports activities activities to make sure their success.

A actual assets business plan is usually a written file that summarizes industrial company possibilities and potentialities and explains how those opportunities can be applied by the usage of using the triumphing team of managers and employees. Writing a real property marketing strategy makes the method of growing it more green, and the plan itself - systematized and concise.

Mastering the art of growing a actual estate business plan is essential for as a minimum the following 5 reasons:

1. The new economic conditions require new marketers and permit them to try to apprehend their "entrepreneurial dispositions". However, lots of these humans have in no way run any business employer and therefore have very little expertise of the whole variety of issues related to entrepreneurship in a market economic gadget;

2. The converting monetary surroundings additionally confronts professional heads of organizations with the need to calculate their destiny steps in a considered certainly one of a kind way and prepare for an uncommon conflict with competition, wherein there ought to be no room for lackluster attitudes.

three. The actual property marketing and marketing approach is the hyperlink amongst you and the investor. If an entrepreneur counts now not nice on his non-public charge range but wants to entice fee variety from outside, that is, to hobby capacity buyers, along with remote places ones, to invest inside the proposed organisation, it is essential to expose them the effectiveness of such an investment. Your potential to count on realistically and test all feasible elements, each immoderate high-quality and horrible, of using the invested price variety.

If you check for the vital price range at a financial company, you can moreover need a actual property advertising and marketing method as a manner to assist persuade the banker of the reliability of the funding, the truth of the move again of the loan issued to you, and the receipt of your income. In this example, the actual assets advertising method is a "available on the market" record to obtain capital. In the "promoting" actual belongings marketing strategy, you need to slightly alternate the emphasis, for instance, ensure to encompass the primary biographical facts of the possible managers, information approximately their schooling and paintings experience. This data is fundamental to capability consumers. Actually, the purpose of a actual assets advertising approach is generally the principle one for absolutely everyone that desires to increase capital. The actual assets advertising technique have to influence traders that the brand new entrepreneur has realistically identified his possibilities, has the entrepreneurial and managerial information to capture those opportunities, and has a reasonably practical, consistent software for generating profits and achieving desires over time.

And in case you do not want borrowed finances? If you have have been given sufficient capital to start your very very own organisation without attracting outdoor investors? Do you want a actual belongings marketing strategy in this situation? In this situation, too, a actual assets advertising and marketing approach is critical. It is vital to cut up methods: making plans and investing. An entrepreneur who has the manner should write a actual belongings advertising approach no longer "in the marketplace", but for himself. In this example, you may acquire the advantages described underneath (fourth, and fifth)

four. The real property marketing strategy will permit, first of all, you to truly see the potentialities of your enterprise business enterprise, check the prevailing economic state of affairs and your opportunities, determine effective guidelines for the development of the company, and all of the vital actions to gain the set goals, study your mind, check them with reasonableness and realism. In this regard, not best the final end result of this planned paintings - an entire actual estate advertising and marketing method but moreover the device of growing a real property business plan itself is valuable. All concerned in it reap an exquisite enjoy of future joint sports activities and verbal exchange, as well as a well-grounded induced view of the possibilities for business enterprise development.

5.   The actual assets advertising and marketing approach will characteristic a stylish for you and your personnel in competition to which you may check the consequences of practical sports for its implementation and make the critical modifications to this hobby. It will permit personnel to honestly understand their duties and word their very personal private possibilities related to a not unusual business employer for all, and test

their contribution to carrying out the set goals. The actual belongings advertising and marketing method will display to be beneficial for putting priorities and man or woman artwork assignments for the number one 3 hundred and sixty five days of the organization.

Consider the superior real property advertising and marketing approach as a "flight map" that defines the maximum applicable, finest in time, and least risky course to accumulate the meant desires.

However, severa factors, along with which includes "surprising climate change" can drastically alternate the plans. For first-timers, it's far common exercise to deviate from the path referred to inside the actual property advertising method. Try to count on possible deviations, extend "fallbacks" and put together "aspect routes". After all, ultimately, it has prolonged been regarded that a plan that doesn't tolerate changes is awful.

Who develops the real belongings advertising and marketing and advertising and marketing approach?

The method to this query can be very short - the primary character (or human beings). The making plans need to be completed thru the usage of the modern-day or destiny leaders of the business enterprise. Then there are folks who will take responsibility for the implementation of the actual property marketing strategy. Let's try to extend our solution and offer an reason behind its specific nature.

The private participation of the pinnacle (modern or capability) in the coaching of the actual belongings marketing approach is so essential that many investors refuse to keep in thoughts packages for the allocation of rate range in any respect if it will become known that the actual property advertising strategy grow to be organized from the start to the cease with the resource of an out of doors representative, and the pinnacle first-rate signed ...

This does not advise, of route, that it isn't crucial to use the services of specialists - pretty the other, the involvement of experts is quite welcomed by manner of customers. However, with the resource of using being concerned on this paintings in my opinion, you type of simulate your future sports activities activities, checking the energy of the plan itself and yourself - will you have got sufficient power to maintain the trouble to a a hit stop and drift on? On the opportunity hand, you show the investor the level of your qualifications, you also are showing your willingness to be entrepreneurial.

If you're uncertain approximately your literary capabilities, ask a person to edit the completed actual property marketing and advertising strategy to accurate grammatical mistakes, but do not keep away from the gadget of creating the real property marketing strategy itself. The time spent on its schooling isn't always wasted: that is the time that you have already dedicated in your future business corporation. You are already operating to your destiny. Developing actual assets corporation plans is exactly what you need to do. Every time you broaden a actual assets advertising strategy, you switch out to be an more and more skilled entrepreneur.

In the machine of making equipped a actual assets advertising and marketing strategy, primarily based at the analysis and calculations completed, you could extensively alternate your initial desire.

Many marketers, no longer being able to kingdom the principle problem, write too much (as plenty as 2 hundred pages). Full of unnecessary records. As a end result, such actual assets enterprise plans are much less effective than they'll be.

Firstly, the excessive amount of the real belongings advertising and marketing method makes it difficult to recognize the essence of the thoughts provided in it, and secondly, this actual assets business plan isn't in all likelihood to be study cautiously.

Consider the problem of familiarizing your self with a hundred-internet page actual estate advertising and marketing method from the mind-set of an investor (in any case, an investor is exactly the person to whom you want to "sell" your real property marketing and advertising and marketing strategy). For severa investment companies, even a medium-sized corporation gets numerous dozen actual belongings commercial enterprise plans every week. How does the possible investor behave in this situation? Four out of five actual assets enterprise company plans can be handed or paused no extra than 10-15 mins after a short test. Of the relaxation, once more 4 out of 5 might be observe a touch greater attentively and longer (an hour or more) and once more located apart. And incredible the relaxation of the general extensive variety of submitted real assets industrial organization plans (approximately one out of a hundred) may be signed and inside the destiny becomes the concern of top notch negotiations, because of which, at great, one of the signed actual estate business agency plans may be invested in.

As for advice, the most fulfilling extent of a real belongings business plan isn't any more than 35-forty pages. Do now not overload it with diagrams and pics for the cause of "analyzing". Use simplest the ones illustrations or diagrams, with out which it is hard to apprehend the content of the actual estate marketing approach. The look of the plan ought to not be an result in itself, the primary detail is the accessibility of records its content material.

And, of route, the real property advertising and advertising approach need to have a come to be privy to net page and a table of contents. The call net internet web page includes the name of the enterprise (or the decision and surname of the capability entrepreneur, if there may be no enterprise however), cope with, e mail address, and cellphone (or fax) variety. It is appropriate to area the desk of contents on one page. This is a completely essential a part of a real estate advertising and marketing method. Each of the readers has his very non-public, the most interesting moments that he wants to right now discover, as an example, the shape of required investments, the timing of their pass again. The desk of contents will right away inform the reader in which to locate this facts. The pages of the actual assets advertising and marketing strategy want to be numbered and placed down next to the names of the sections within the desk of contents.

Components of your real assets advertising method

Real property organization plans start from the quit – with a summary. This is a crucial part of your actual assets marketing method. For many real property industrial organisation plans that is the handiest section so that it will be have a look at with the aid of using a ability investor, and then the actual estate marketing method can be positioned apart. This manner that the "short conclusions" have to grow to be unconvincing and not hobby the investor. Summaries permit the reader to recognize the number one thoughts and possibilities of your commercial organization rapid and determine whether or not or now not or no longer to spend the extra time studying your plan. Consequently, the reason of short conclusions (summaries) is to interest or maybe "seduce" the capability reader.

To try this, you should be capable of supply your optimism within the course of your business agency to the reader. To try this, you do not need to apply "slogans", in fact display screen in a benevolent, non-public tone which you are geared up and capable of use all the possibilities furnished via the market to gain success.

Summary conclusions are the essence of your concept, that is the cease end result of an already written real property business plan. Here, on one or (most 3) pages, the essence of your business corporation want to be presented in a clearly easy and concise way: what are you going to do, how your destiny product (issuer) will range from competitors' merchandise and why consumers may be interested in it, what expenses (investments) can be required for the implementation of your assignment and belongings in their receipt. Here you need to offer digital facts at the quantity of future income (in the subsequent three-five years), earnings, income, the quantity of profitability, and, in the long run, the duration at some point of which you can be confident to move again all borrowed funds (or in other phrases, the payback length of the capital funding).

As follows from the contents of the "Brief Conclusions", they, of course, are written after the actual belongings advertising method is honestly prepared, all its sections are calculated, and you, together on the facet of your personnel and involved professionals, have performed whole readability in all the data of your venture. Depending on the character of your enterprise and the abilities of the writer, you may put together forms of summary conclusions: concise or descriptive.

Concise summary conclusions are more honest and "frank" for 2 motives: they simply repeat in abbreviated shape the conclusions of every segment of the real property advertising technique. The benefit of such brief conclusions is that they will be easy to install writing and are least dependent on the functionality of the author. The pleasant downside of concise precis conclusions is a too "dry", commercial enterprise enterprise tone. The government summary covers all sections of your real property marketing strategy and gives them in addition, albeit abbreviated.

Brief descriptive conclusions are like a brief tale which you gift to the reader. Here you may describe your commercial employer with super drama and pleasure. However, it is important to have 'sufficient capacity to provide the specified statistics, arouse the passion of the reader and not fall into exaggeration. With those succinct summaries, you can evoke an emotional reaction from the reader with the useful useful resource of mentioning one or of the maximum extremely good trends of your organization and showing how those dispositions will make contributions to the achievement of your destiny commercial enterprise.

The order of presentation of the fabric inside the short precis is bigoted. In this case, for example, the concept of your agency may be defined in three paragraphs, and the manage group - in one or   sentences. It all relies upon on what you pay extra attention to. They have to, however, give your buyers all the information they need.

In precis...

- Consider the evolved actual belongings advertising and marketing approach as a "flight map" that defines the maximum suitable, maximum green in time, and least unstable path to achieve the supposed desires. However, it is vital to have sufficient ability on the equal time as offering the desired information, arousing the keenness of the reader and not falling into exaggeration.

Chapter 9: Introduction to Making Money in Real Estate

Congratulations on Picking Up This Book!

My name is,the us's critical expert on flipping houses for quick cash. After flipping masses of gives all over the united states of the us and training heaps of human beings similar to you the way to effectively do the identical, I'd want to introduce to you a actual property method for making short cash without proudly proudly owning, dealing with, renovating, and if achieved efficiently, whilst now not having any cash!

What am I Talking About?

I'm talking approximately a actual property flipping technique called "wholesaling." The purpose of this e-book is to be your pass-to manual to correctly wholesale houses earning $three,000 to $10,000 in keeping with deal on common.

What is Wholesaling?

There are numerous specific techniques to explain wholesaling. Here are some...

•Wholesaling is the method of obtaining distressed homes at a discount after which passing those offers off to a few other investor for a fee.

•Wholesaling is buying low and selling low.

•Wholesaling is getting paid for finding proper offers for rehabbers and buy-and-maintain customers for a rate.

•Wholesaling is getting a deal underneath settlement and then assigning the settlement to three other investor for a charge.

All of these definitions are correct however the most important distinction to recognize in terms of flipping houses is that wholesaling in NOT doing any upgrades to the assets (known as rehabbing or healing and turn). It's passing the deal off to someone else who will do the upgrades.

Essentially, wholesaling is taking an awful lot much less earnings now and not using a piece (now not doing any enhancements) in preference to greater earnings later with an entire lot of paintings (doing enhancements and flipping it or renting it).

Wholesalers are in immoderate demand in every market. Most customers pick no longer having to spend the time finding actual deals and will gladly pay wholesalers to discover and produce them true gives.

Why Wholesaling?

Not most effective is wholesaling the remarkable method for buying began in actual belongings but it's also the first rate manner to make extra money, duration.

Here's why... on the equal time as finished effectively (and following my techniques said in this ebook), wholesaling doesn't require any coins or credit. There is genuinely no risk on your aspect and I am however to appearance an less difficult manner to make $three,000 to $10,000. Regardless of your financial dreams and whether or no longer you make a decision to go directly to fantastic actual belongings making an funding techniques which consist of rentals, rehabs, hire alternatives, new introduction, notes, even commercial, there will continuously be an possibility to speedy wholesale a property, make a short income, and float at once to some exceptional deal.

Is Wholesaling for You?

Learning a way to wholesale homes is for you if...

-You want to make some extra cash aspect-time to your spare time

-You need to do real estate whole time and fireside your boss

-You want to work from home, be your personal boss and create your private time desk

-You need extra time and freedom to do what you want, whilst you want to do it

-You're bored with scrimping and slightly getting by means of way of way of

-You want more money to adventure, eat at nice consuming locations and feature wonderful matters

-You don't need to deal with rehabbing houses and babysitting contractors

-You don't need to deal with tenants, toilets and turnover

-You want to make money in real assets but you don't have investment capital or credit score to fund deals

-You need to perform a little element amusing, interesting and worthwhile

-You just like the concept of getting paid on your efforts

-You similar to the idea of not having a ceiling on how a whole lot cash you could make

-You want extra money to attend to your ageing mother and father or located your kids via college

-You're involved approximately retirement and need to have a nest egg

-You're sick and uninterested within the nine to 5 rat race, administrative center politics and rush hour visitors

-You truly need to offer your self and your family a higher future

-You want to create a legacy for generations to go back

Ultimately, wholesaling and this e book are for you in case you need extra time and freedom to be, do, have and provide what's in truth essential to you in your life.

The Good News...

Here's the coolest news...You can correctly learn how to find out and wholesale offers from domestic in your spare time with none cash or credit score rating score even in case you've by no means carried out a real property deal earlier than than! Just observe the strategies and gadget stated in this ebook and you could begin earning on common $3,000 to $10,000 in step with deal (or more).

Who Am I and Why Should You Listen to Me?

You may be thinking who's and why should I concentrate to him?

-I've correctly flipped masses of offers definitely in the past 10 years

-I own and characteristic a multi-million dollar national house flipping enterprise

-I'm the owner and CEO of Flipping Mastery, which has been education, instructing, mentoring or perhaps partnering with regular people while you consider that 1997

Simply positioned...I apprehend what I'm speakme about and can help you be successful!

My Story...

It wasn't typically that manner. I grew up in rural Michigan in a farmhouse constructed inside the late 1800s with my parents and six siblings. When my dad offered the residence, it didn't surely have going for walks water. My brothers and I chopped firewood to warm temperature the residence with a wood burning range. I wasn't born with any unique privileges. We struggled financially but fortunately I even have turn out to be raised in a loving domestic and my dad taught me the price of difficult work.

Later, as a newly married husband, father and agency, I supported my family as an underground production employee. I labored for a software excavating corporation and my process changed into to manually dig holes. Imagine this… It's raining and bloodless. An excavator is digging a hole 10 toes deep and encounters a water or sewer pipe. Someone has to get down in that hollow with a shovel to carefully dig for the duration of the water or sewer pipe as a manner to not damage it. That end up my assignment!

It come to be backbreaking work and I can also come home ordinary so filthy grimy from digging holes all day that my wife may want to make me take my closes off on the porch earlier than coming inner. We have been so awful that my co-people may also make a laugh of me due to the reality for lunch my sandwich had best a unmarried slice of cheese. With small kids at home, we couldn't find the money for lunchmeat. Everyday I notion about a better manner but I didn't have pretty a few opportunities in my existence so I didn't recognize wherein to show.

Then in some unspecified time in the future my whole life modified. A buddy invited me to attend a real property investing seminar with him. I borrowed the coins and went. At that seminar I found out some vital techniques approximately wholesaling (which I've considering the fact that perfected).

I became so excited and without a preceding experience or cash, in my spare time in advance than and after my manufacturing assignment, I began wholesaling junker houses in Detroit. After awhile, I have become capable of quite my way and wholesale homes whole time.

Now I'm going to be honest with you. I made an entire lot of mistakes. I didn't have the strategies and gadget that I've mentioned in detail on this ebook. It wasn't until I were given a a fulfillment mentor, a person who had finished what I have become looking to do, that I in reality started to gather achievement.

That became decrease lower back in 2005. Since then I've executed loads of wholesale offers and I've done pretty much each actual belongings making an funding method to be had however my roots have normally been wholesaling. Even these days, in most instances, if I could make a short wholesale charge on a deal while not having to renovate or control it, I'll do this on every occasion!

Remember, "A fowl in hand is higher than in the bush."

In different terms, often, it's better to make $10,000 on a wholesale deal right now without any work, attempt or capital, then potentially $25,000 in a hundred and twenty days after I recovery it up and sell it.

Why I Wrote This Book.

As a entire-time real belongings investor I'm regularly requested why I wrote this ebook and my extraordinary real belongings making an funding books. There are reasons.

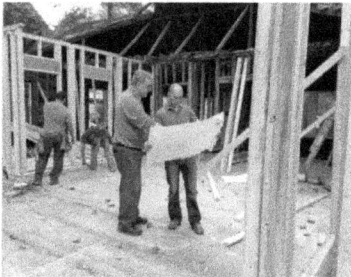

The first reason is self-serving. I carry out a nationwide business business enterprise solving and flipping houses all in the route of the usa and I'm continuously looking for correct offers that I can recuperation and turn for earnings. Most of my gives come from wholesalers like you. In reality, in case you're inquisitive about incomes

$10,000 constant with deal for every residence you convey me that suits my requirements, then go to: www.PowerFlipper3x.Com to investigate more.

The 2nd motive is to assist human beings benefit financial safety. When I began out I become broke and felt trapped in a dull give up pastime. I made a dedication to God that if he may additionally bless me with prosperity, I may also supply lower back and educate others what I've determined out.

I'm happy to document that through my books and education applications and mentoring, I've been able to assist hundreds of people similar to you. Whether it's making more money component-time or quitting their jobs and turning into whole-time real property entrepreneurs or going from doing 10 offers a 12 months to doing 50 gives a yr, the cause of this ebook is to offer you the abilties and self assure to acquire your economic goals.

Whatever your motive for choosing up this book, without a doubt don't forget...

It's not approximately the cash. It's approximately having the TIME and FREEDOM to HAVE, BE, DO and GIVE the whole thing you need in existence.

What You Can Expect From This Book:

My aim in penning this ebook is to offer you an intensive facts of the manner to wholesale residential houses so you ought to have the abilties, know-how and comprehend-the way to straight away start imposing the wholesale approach and begin making $3,000 to $10,000 on commonplace steady with deal.

You'll discover ways to discover correct wholesale offers and the way to placed those offers together. You'll have a look at the popular wholesale acquisition timeline and technique. You'll learn how to dominate a market, how to investigate and form gives, and a way to continuously locate offers similarly to clients to turn them to. Most importantly, you'll learn how to create a pipeline to typically do gives.

Additional Resources: To get my complete device for flipping houses which consist of all my locating, analyzing, tracking and manage device, workplace work and software program software, go to www.ResultsNow.Com

How to Use This Book:

This ebook is designed to be a guidebook. Throughout its pages you'll see severa examples and what I name "breakout sessions" in that you'll have the opportunity to practice the technique being taught. Take those breakout sessions considerably as they may ensure which you're greedy the necessities efficiently.

This ebook is damaged down into six foremost regions of interest:

1.Understanding Your Target Market: There are three awesome kinds of consumers to wholesale homes to.

2.Analyzing Deals: Being able to calculate the numbers to decide the right purchase price so you could make a earnings wholesaling it to some exceptional investor.

three.Controlling Deals: How to properly located offers together with stimulated dealers and coins customers.

four.Finding Deals: How to constantly locate inspired sellers and discounted offers to your market.

5.Finding Cash Buyers: How we discover close by cash clients to your goal marketplace which might be seeking out deals.

6.Funding Deals: If and at the same time as wanted, a way to fund wholesale gives.

Wholesaling Timeline:

There are six steps to doing a wholesale deal that we'll communicate in this ebook...

1. Find a deal

2. Get it below settlement (manage)

3. Find a consumer

4. Assign your settlement to the stylish customer

five. Close at the deal

6. Cash your check and have a high-quality time!

The timeline from whilst you discover a deal to cashing the take a look at can take anywhere from a few days to 30 days or greater depending on how speedy you may do the six steps.

Myths and Realities About Wholesaling:

There are numerous not unusual myths or misconceptions about wholesaling. Here are some...

•Myth: It's unlawful.

•Reality: It's no longer unlawful as long as the deal is established properly.

•Myth: It takes quite a few cash.

•Reality: It is based totally upon on the way you shape the deal. I'll display you a manner to shape offers with out using any coins.

•Myth: It's time eating.

•Reality: Wholesaling is the fastest manner to make coins in real belongings due to the reality you're no longer proudly owning or handling the offers.

•Myth: Everyone is doing it.

•Reality: Most investors want offers but aren't inclined to place in the attempt to find out suitable gives, making wholesalers high in call for.

•Myth: Mistakes are magnified and costly.

•Realty: If mounted well and due to the fact you're not proudly owning or managing the homes, wholesaling is the least volatile investment approach.

•Myth: There are not any offers.

•Reality: There are generally gives. You genuinely need to recognize a manner to discover them.

•Myth: There aren't any buyers to wholesale to.

•Reality: There are continuously shoppers searching out offers. You truely need to apprehend a way to locate them.

Throughout this ebook, I will debunk all of these myths and display you a clean roadmap to constantly and profitably wholesale offers.

Commonly Used Acronyms:

Throughout this ebook I'll use numerous acronyms not unusual to wholesaling and real assets. Here's a short listing to refer to:

•REO: Bank owned belongings. It's prolonged beyond through foreclosures, and the financial group took it lower once more and now is trying to sell it.

•MLS: Multiple Listing Service. The MLS is a collaboration belongings posting provider in which real belongings sellers put up their houses.

•ROI: Return on Investment.

•ARV: After Repair Value. The rate of a assets as quickly because it's constant up.

•LLC: Limited Liability Company. A jail entity form.

•COMPING: The technique of figuring out the ARV of a topic belongings via analyzing supplied, lively and pending similar homes.

Chapter 10: Understanding Your Target Market

Understanding Market Trends:

First and essential, it's very critical as a wholesaler to understand the how markets shift and the way those shifts have an impact on pricing and in the end your capability to wholesale offers.

Buyer's Market:

A patron's market is even as the deliver of houses is greater than the call for of customers (deliver is up, call for is down). When a marketplace is a "consumer's market" and supply is up but name for is down, the price of houses drops due to the fact there are too few customers chasing too many houses.

Seller's Market:

The contrary of a purchaser's marketplace is a what's known as a "seller's market." A company's marketplace is in reality the opportunity; Supply (homes) is down and communicate to for (shoppers) is up. When a marketplace is a "seller's market" and deliver is down but name for is up, the rate of homes goes up due to the fact there are too many clients chasing now not sufficient homes.

The natural development of real estate is for markets to variety from a consumer's market to a dealer's market primarily based on deliver and speak to for (till the government interferes, it virtually is some one-of-a-kind story). Keep in thoughts, after I say "marketplace," I will be referring to the complete U.S., all the way right all the way down to the u . S . A ., county, city, network or even street.

Remember, your achievement as a wholesaler ultimately comes all the manner down to your ability to recognize market values and a way to adjust your attempting to find method because the marketplace shifts up an down.

Understanding the Three Target Buyers:

When it entails wholesaling deals, there are 3 one in all a type aim clients to wholesale homes to.

1.Fix and Flip Investor: An investor who buys houses, fixes them up and re-sells them to a retail purchaser (property owner) for a profits.

2.Buy and Hold Investor: An investor who buys houses, fixes them up and maintains them to lease out for prolonged-time period cash go with the go with the flow.

3.Retail Buyer: The give up purchaser or proprietor of a house seeking out a discount with the aim of buying a deal and solving it up themselves.

Your wholesaling method varies substantially relying on which of the three shoppers you are wholesaling offers to. You need to understand your aim client by way of the use of the use of developing a niche and then dominating that region of hobby. The higher you apprehend your patron and what sorts of deals he or she desires, the greater a success you'll be.

Let's smash down the anatomy of each of the three clients.

Fix and Flip Investor:

A restore and flip investor buys distressed houses, fixes them up after which re-sells them to retail customers (owners). This shape of investor focuses on regions that have robust retail values (appropriate schools, purchasing, downtown, and so forth). Some attention on first-time customer markets, at the equal time as others focus on better profits markets. Some popularity on very moderate renovations (carpet and paint), at the identical time as others do complete blown rehabs (replace the whole lot).

Again, your process as a wholesaler is to discover the sort of healing and turn investor you need to serve and then find them offers that in shape their looking for criteria.

Fix and Flip Buy Formula:

In addition to records the kind of retail patron the restore and turn investor flips to and the shape of rehabs they do, it's vital you apprehend their purchase machine so you realize what price you need to get offers underneath agreement at, so that you can upload for your wholesale rate.

Most repair and turn traders follow what's known as "The sixty 5% Formula." Here's the way it works...

Step 1: Determine ARV: First a recovery and flip investor will determine the After Repair Value (ARV), this is the fee the residence will promote for to a retail customer as fast as improvements have been made (more on ARV later).

Step 2: Subtract Desired Profit, Estimated Closing Fees and Cost of Capital: Most traders use 35% of ARV to cowl those 3 topics. Here's the breakdown.

Desired Profit: A wholesome earnings most restore and flip consumers goal for is 20% of ARV. This of course is the proper deal and allows for some room in case the deal doesn't education session flawlessly.

Estimated Closing Costs: Every recovery and flip investor has costs to buy a belongings and once more to sell the belongings which includes escrow, call insurance, recordings, commissions, property tax, and plenty of others. A healthful amount to detail in is 10% of ARV.

Cost of Capital: Most repair and turn traders use financing to cowl the purchase and/or renovations and want to "deliver" the loan or financing till the property sells. A wholesome quantity to element in is five% of ARV.

Since those 3 topics are taken into consideration "ordinary" and every repair and flip investor must trouble them in, the same old rule is to genuinely take 35% proper off of the pinnacle from the ARV. In other phrases, if the ARV is $3 hundred,000 then 35% or $a hundred and five,000 need to be factored in to cover profits, last charges and fee of capital.

Step 3: Subtract Repair Cost: The zero.33 step is to issue in the charge of renovation. This range is not consistent, as every deal will need specific protection to make it "retail-prepared" (constant up and prepared to promote to a proprietor of a residence).

Once you've achieved the ones 3 steps, you're capable of calculate the restore and flip purchase charge. Here is a clean system to examine:

(ARV x .Sixty five) – Repairs = Fix and Flip Buy Price

**Note: Multiplying ARV x .Sixty five is a quick reduce to subtracting 35% from ARV

In order to calculate the Fix and Flip sixty five% Formula you need to understand topics:

1.ARV and

2.Repairs

Example #1:

So allow's look at an example. Let's count on that a deal has an ARV of $three hundred,000 and the upkeep are $fifty five,000. What is the acquisition rate?

(ARV x .Sixty five) – Repairs = Fix and Flip Buy Price

$3 hundred,000 x .Sixty 5) – $fifty five,000 = Fix and Flip Buy Price

$195,000 - $fifty 5,000

$140,000 = Fix and Flip Buy Price

Answer Example #1:

First take $three hundred,000 x .65 = $195,000. Then $195,000 - $fifty five,000 in protection = $140,000 purchase price. So in this situation, a restoration and turn investor should purchase this specific deal for $a hundred and forty,000. So as a wholesaler, getting this deal anywhere beneath $140,000 is your charge. If you have got been capable of get this deal under agreement for, permit's say, $130,000, you may be able to wholesale it to a repair and flip investor for $a hundred and forty,000 and make $10,000!

Wholesale Fix and Fix Formula:

(ARV x .Sixty 5) – Repairs – Wholesale Fee = Wholesale Buy Price

Let's perform a little breakout durations to ensure you apprehend the healing and flip purchase approach.

Breakout Session #1:

ARV: $235,000

Repairs: $42,000

Wholesale Fee: $7,000

What is the purchase fee?

_____

_____

_____

_____

Breakout Session #1 Answer:

(ARV x .Sixty 5) — Repairs — Wholesale Fee = Wholesale Buy Price

$235,000 x .Sixty 5) — $forty two,000 - $7,000 = Wholesale Buy Price

$152,750 - $42,000 - $7,000 = Wholesale Buy Price

$103,750 = Wholesale Buy Price

Breakout Session #2:

ARV: $100 twenty five,000

Repairs: $20,000

Wholesale Fee: $five,000

What is the acquisition charge?

_____

_____

_____

Breakout Session #2 Answer:

(ARV x .Sixty five) − Repairs − Wholesale Fee = Wholesale Buy Price

$one hundred twenty five,000 x .Sixty 5) − $20,000 - $5,000 = Wholesale Buy Price

$eighty one,250 - $20,000 - $5,000 = Wholesale Buy Price

$56,250 = Wholesale Buy Price

Breakout Session #3:

ARV: $375,000

Repairs: $70,000

Wholesale Fee: $10,000

What is the acquisition fee?

_____

_____

_____

_____

Breakout Session #three Answer:

(ARV x .65) – Repairs – Wholesale Fee = Wholesale Buy Price

$375,000 x .Sixty five) – $70,000 - $10,000 = Wholesale Buy Price

$243,750 - $70,000 - $10,000 = Wholesale Buy Price

$163,750 = Wholesale Buy Price

Buy and Hold Investor

The 2nd shape of investor to bear in mind wholesaling deals to is a buy and maintain investor. A purchase and hold investor buys homes with the motive to maintain lengthy-term and rent for cash drift. They look at their corporation absolutely in a completely unique way than a restoration and flipper does. They have a look at offers primarily based on an annual price of move back or internet walking earnings (NOI). In other phrases, how a high-quality deal cash flow can they earn?

Cap Rate Formula: Analyzing offers based definitely mostly on cap price is generally used with business making an funding but is also common with unmarried-own family residential homes. Cap charge is the price of pass decrease lower back based totally completely mostly on the profits that the property is expected to generate. It's used to estimate the investor's potential go back on his or her investment (ROI). For instance, if a property earns $10,000 in annual net profits and the cost to accumulate the assets (capital funding) is $a hundred,000, then the cap charge is 10, or in special terms, the ROI is 10%.

Wholesaling Cap Rate Formula:

There are four simple steps to wholesaling a deal to a buy and hold investor who makes use of cap price to shop for gives.

Step 1: Determine Net Operating Income (NOI): NOI is actually your internet earnings after subtracting all of the working expenses which includes upkeep, emptiness, belongings taxes, belongings manipulate, and so forth from the gross earnings. So if hire is $800/month and strolling prices are $500/month, the NOI is $three hundred/month.

Step 2: Determine Investor's Desired Cap Rate: You want to discover what the desired cap fee is for buyers. As a favored rule of thumb, a 10-cap is fashionable however, the more volatile the investment, the higher the popular cap rate and the extra constant the funding, the decrease the cap price.

Step three: Determine Investor's Total Capital Investment: Once you recognize the projected annual NOI and the investor's cap price, you can calculate their conventional capital funding. This is achieved through taking NOI / Cap Rate = capital investment: For instance, if the every year NOI is $5,000 and the cap fee is 10, then you genuinely take $5,000 / .10 which equals $50,000. In specific terms, if the investor spends a whole of $50,000 to build up the assets that produces $five,000/three hundred and sixty five days NOI, he is going to earn a 10% ROI.

Step four: Determine Wholesale Buy Price: Once you understand the investor's capital investment, subtract out renovation and wholesale rate. For instance, if the general capital funding is $50,000 and preservation are $15,000 and the wholesale fee is $5,000, then the purchase fee is $30,000. ($50,000 - $15,000 - $5,000).

Example #1:

So permit's have a have a study an example. Let's suppose that a deal has gross rents of $1,500/month with $800/month in operating charges and the investor's cap fee is 7.

What is the wholesale buy fee if you favored to earn a $9,000 wholesale charge and upkeep are $17,500?

Step 1: Determine Net Operating Income (NOI):

Annual gross income – annual usual taking walks prices

$1,500 x 3 hundred and sixty 5 days = $18,000 annual gross income.

$800 x one year = $nine,600 annual operating fees

$18,000 - $nine,six hundred = $eight,four hundred annual NOI

Step 2: Determine Investor's Desired Cap Rate:

In this situation we're using a cap fee of 7.

Step three: Determine Investor's Total Capital Investment:

NOI / Cap Rate = Total Capital Investment

$eight,400 / .07 = $100 twenty,000 capital funding

Step 4: Determine Wholesale Buy Price:

Capital investment – maintenance – wholesale rate = wholesale purchase fee

$a hundred twenty,000 - $17,500 - $nine,000 = $ninety 3,500 wholesale buy price

So if you purchased this deal beneath agreement for $90 3,500, you may wholesale it for $102,500 ($nine,000 charge) to this investor, who will spend $17,500 on enhancements after which lease it out for $1,500 month and earn a nine-cap rate at the investment.

Once you've finished the ones 4 steps, you're capable of calculate the wholesale cap fee purchase fee. Here is a clean approach to conform with:

(NOI / Cap Rate) – Repairs – Wholesale Fee = Wholesale Buy Price

Let's do a few breakout instructions to ensure you recognize the method for wholesaling to cap fee purchase and hold buyers.

Breakout Session #four:

Annual NOI = $10,000

Cap Rate = eleven

Repairs = $eleven,000

Wholesale Fee: $7,000

What is the wholesale buy charge?

_____

_____

_____

_____

Breakout Session #four Answer:

(NOI / Cap Rate) – Repairs – Wholesale Fee = Wholesale Buy Price

($10,000 / .11) - $11,000 - $7,000 = Wholesale Buy Price

$90,909 – $11,000 – $7,000 = Wholesale Buy Price

= $72,909 Wholesale Buy Price

www.ingramcontent.com/pod-product-compliance
Lightning Source LLC
Chambersburg PA
CBHW071222210326
41597CB00016B/1907